# THE

# EVERYTHING KIDS'®

# WORD SEARCH PUZZLE AND ACTIVITY BOOK

Solve clever clues and hunt for hidden words in 100 mind-bending puzzles

Beth L. Blair and Jennifer A. Ericsson

**A**adamsmedia

Avon, Massachusetts

DIRECTOR OF INNOVATION  Paula Munier

EDITORIAL DIRECTOR  Laura M. Daly

EXECUTIVE EDITOR, SERIES BOOKS  Brielle K. Matson

ASSOCIATE COPY CHIEF  Sheila Zwiebel

ACQUISITIONS EDITOR  Kerry Smith

DEVELOPMENT EDITOR  Katie McDonough

PRODUCTION EDITOR  Casey Ebert

. . . . . . . . . . . . . . . . . . . . . . . . .

An Everything® Series Book.
Everything® and everything.com® are registered trademarks of F+W Media, Inc.

Published by Adams Media, a division of F+W Media, Inc.
57 Littlefield Street, Avon, MA 02322. U.S.A.
*www.adamsmedia.com*

ISBN-10: 1-59869-545-2
ISBN-13: 978-1-59869-545-8

Printed by RR Donnelley, Owensville, MO, US

10  9  8  7  6  5  4  3

March 2010

This publication is designed to provide accurate and authoritative information with regard to the subject matter covered. It is sold with the understanding that the publisher is not engaged in rendering legal, accounting, or other professional advice. If legal advice or other expert assistance is required, the services of a competent professional person should be sought.
—From a *Declaration of Principles* jointly adopted by a Committee of the American Bar Association and a Committee of Publishers and Associations

Many of the designations used by manufacturers and sellers to distinguish their products are claimed as trademarks. When those designations appear in this book and Adams Media was aware of a trademark claim, the designations have been printed with initial capital letters.

Cover illustrations by Dana Regan.
Interior illustrations by Kurt Dolber.
Puzzles by Beth L. Blair.

*This book is available at quantity discounts for bulk purchases.*
*For information, please call 1-800-289-0963.*

# Contents

# DEDICATION

To Katie B.—
May you always find the right words!
Love, Aunt Jenny

To my Daddy-O, who is never at a loss
for just the right words.

Beth

# Introduction

**W**elcome to *The Everything® KIDS' Word Search Puzzle and Activity Book!* The word search—which is essentially a game of hide-and-seek with letters—is a great puzzle. Word searches can be simple to do, but they are more satisfying if there is a twist or two added. In this book, you'll find some basic searches, but a lot of the puzzles also have an added element of fun!

A basic word search has a list of words and a letter grid. Your job is to locate all the listed words, which are hidden in the grid. Easy, right? Not always! Look at the sample puzzle. It shows that the words can be hiding in several different directions. Words can overlap each other, too.

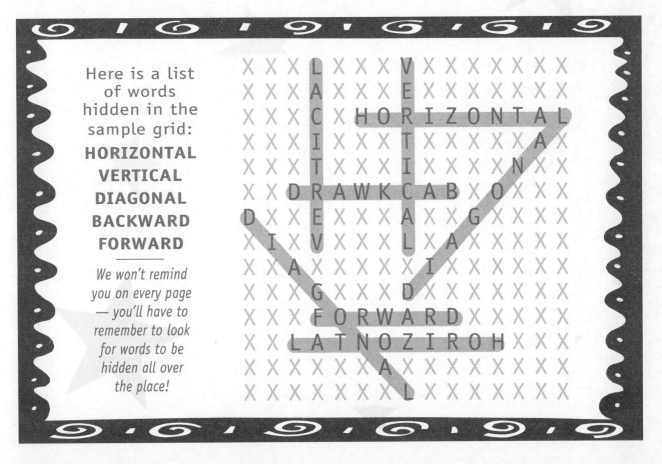

Here is a list of words hidden in the sample grid:

**HORIZONTAL**
**VERTICAL**
**DIAGONAL**
**BACKWARD**
**FORWARD**

*We won't remind you on every page — you'll have to remember to look for words to be hidden all over the place!*

Every once in a while, the words will be placed in the grid in a different pattern. You might have to look for words that are spelled in a circle or curve through the puzzle like a snake. We'll certainly let you know about these special puzzles in their directions!

Once you have located a word in the grid, you'll want to mark it in some way. Some people use a pencil or pen to draw a big loop around the whole word. Personally, we like to use highlighting markers and draw a line of bright pink, yellow, orange, or blue right through the word. This makes the answers pop right off the page!

You might be wondering if there is a best way to approach a word search. We've found that some people move systematically through the puzzle, searching across or up and down each line. Other people look for the uncommon letters first—like J or Q—that might not appear too often in the grid. You can try these methods out, or look for one that suits you better.

We have tried to add a little extra fun into these puzzles. You might need to unscramble letters, break a code, or solve picture clues to get the word list for that puzzle. For others, there's a hidden picture or joke in the grid when you're done. Some of the puzzles do not come with a word list, and in others words are hiding more than once. We've tried to mix it up so that each word search puzzle will be fresh and exciting.

What are you waiting for? Start searching!

Beth L. Blair
Jennifer A. Ericsson

# Chapter 1

# Around the House

# Dynamic Duos

There are some foods that we always seem to eat together!

Find one edible item in the upper word search, and then figure out its "companion" food in the lower word search. On the next page, you'll find spaces to write in the mystery foods.

```
X M M I L K K H A M J S
S S T K T X O Q K W X T
P E A N U T B U T T E R
A W J Q D X J R G S J A
G J Q O G W T K E G J W
H E G G S T J E T A G B
E S J T G Q H K Q P D E
T X W B A C A N G P G R
T J K Q G K W X G L X R
I W X L E T T U C E G I
R K J W J Q T Q T S J E
S F R E N C H F R I E S
```

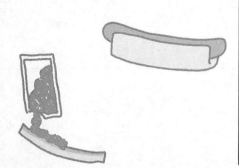

```
X C O O K I E S J J G C
S K R Y J K G H E Y K R
R M E A T B A L L S U E
E G J H C Q E J L Q K A
G H J G H K S K Y H J M
R J H Y H E E H U K S M
U Q B U T T E R J G E G
B Q G Y H C H H S I G H
M A Q K G H C H Q K N Y
A K C K J U H Y K G A H
H Y H O H P H J Y H R Y
G H Q G N K O T A M O T
```

E _ _ _ _ & B _ _ _ _ _

M _ _ _ _ & C _ _ _ _ _ _ _

B _ _ _ _ _ & B _ _ _ _ _

A _ _ _ _ _ _ & O _ _ _ _ _ _

P _ _ _ _ _ _ _ _ _ _ _ _ & J _ _ _ _ _

S _ _ _ _ _ _ _ _ _ _ & M _ _ _ _ _ _ _ _

C _ _ _ _ _ _ & C _ _ _ _ _ _ _ _

S _ _ _ _ _ _ _ _ _ _ _ _ & _ _ _ _ _ _

L _ _ _ _ _ _ & _ _ _ _ _ _

H _ _ & C _ _ _ _ _ _

F _ _ _ _ _ _ _ _ _ _ & K _ _ _ _ _ _

H _ _ _ _ _ _ _ & H _ _ _ _ _ _ _ _

CREAM

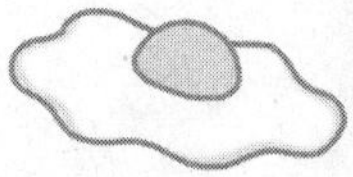

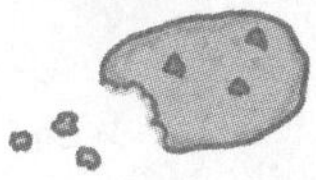

# Lotsa Laundry

Mom threw a load of white laundry into the washing machine. Oh no! One piece of red clothing got mixed in by mistake. It will turn everything pink! Use a pink marker to highlight all the clothes in the washing machine.

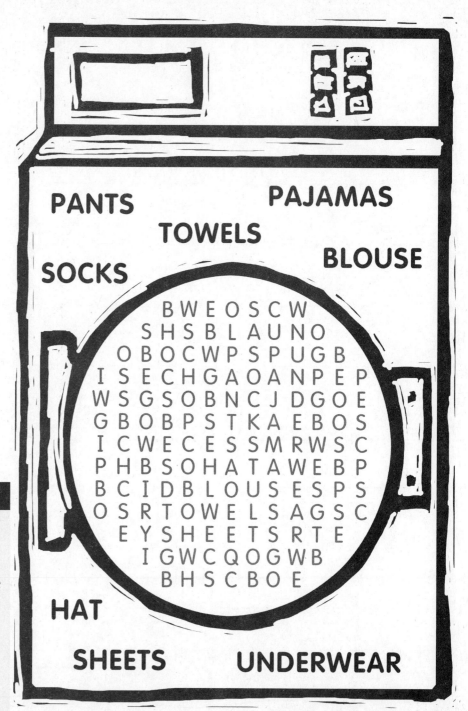

PANTS

PAJAMAS

TOWELS

SOCKS

BLOUSE

```
B W E O S C W
S H S B L A U N O
O B O C W P S P U G B
I S E C H G A O A N P E P
W S G S O B N C J D G O E
G B O B P S T K A E B O S
I C W E C E S S M R W S C
P H B S O H A T A W E B P
B C I D B L O U S E S P S
O S R T O W E L S A G S C
E Y S H E E T S R T E
I G W C Q O G W B
B H S C B O E
```

HAT

SHEETS

UNDERWEAR

**Extra Fun:**

Now use the marker to highlight the letters in the word L-A-U-N-D-R-Y. Once you have finished, look at the pattern you have made. You will see which piece of clothing turned the laundry pink!

# Cutting the Cake

The birthday girl has to cut pieces of cake for all of her guests. Look carefully inside the cake for the twelve people on the list who came to celebrate!

| | |
|---|---|
| MOTHER | UNCLE |
| FATHER | GRANDMA |
| SISTER | GRANDPA |
| BROTHER | FRIEND |
| COUSIN | NEIGHBOR |
| AUNT | CLASSMATE |

**Added Fun:** The letters B-I-R-T-H-D-A-Y G-I-R-L form a small rectangle somewhere in the cake—the birthday girl's name will be inside of it!

```
C L A S S M A T E O F U T F
E F T S R O B H G I E N O T
G R A N D M A M J F S C F U
R I E S O F U E O J S L A F
A E U H J E O F K T U E T S
N N E O T J B I R T H J H E
D D T F U O L A M Y D E E T
P S I S T E R I G Y A J R O
A U N T F S S B E O F E U F
    N I S U O C U E
```

The birthday girl's name is:

# Trail of Toys

The kids in this house sure need to pick up their stuff! First, look at the picture and circle eleven things the kids have been playing with. Then highlight the names of those items in the letter grid. Look carefully: Answers can go backwards and diagonally too!

```
L J A E T A K S E C I
L A T E D D Y B E A R
A C R J U R M A P R O
B K U P E U S L L O D
E S C E A M K L N D B
S O K I T E S O K A O
A I T E N N I O O S X
B N C R A Y O N S B B
```

# Bathroom Humor

Find all the items listed below in the grid. Read the remaining letters from left to right and top to bottom to find a funny bathroom joke!

**BATHTUB**
**SHOWER**
**MIRROR**
**TOILET**
**SINK**
**THERMOMETER**
**TOOTHBRUSH**
~~LAUNDRY BASKET~~
**TISSUES**
**TOOTHPASTE**
**WATER**
**HAIRBRUSH**
**SOAP**
**SHAMPOO**
**COMB**
**CUP**
**TOWELS**
**TOYS**
**FLOSS**
**BATHMAT**
~~MEDICINE CABINET~~

```
L W T H O S R O R R I M
A H O T O I L E T T O E
U S Y A P N L W A H H D
N U S Y M K S S T E A I
D R E A A L S T H R I C
R B U T H T A B P M R I
Y H S E S S O A A O B N
B T H S P I O T N M R E
A O O T O S H H E E U C
S O W B C L A M T T S A
K T E H U E F A R E H B
E B R O P W A T E R O I
T M M ? R O O B B E R N
D U T O O T H P A S T E
C K Y ! C S E U S S I T
```

Eight words are listed below. These are NOT the words you will be looking for in the puzzle. You must think of a rhyming word for each one that might make a perfect pet—then look for these animals in the letter grid!

**Extra Fun:** After you have found all the pets, read the remaining letters from left to right and top to bottom. You will find the name of one pet for which there is no rhyme!

```
M  O  U  S  E
H  S  I  F  T
O  B  I  R  D
R  U  T  U  R
S  N  A  K  E
E  N  C  T  L
E  Y  D  O  G
```

Words to Rhyme:        Pets to Look For:

**WORD** _____

**HAT** _____

**FORCE** _____

**ACHE** _____

**HOUSE** _____

**LOG** _____

**WISH** _____

**MONEY** _____

*Extra Letter Pet:*

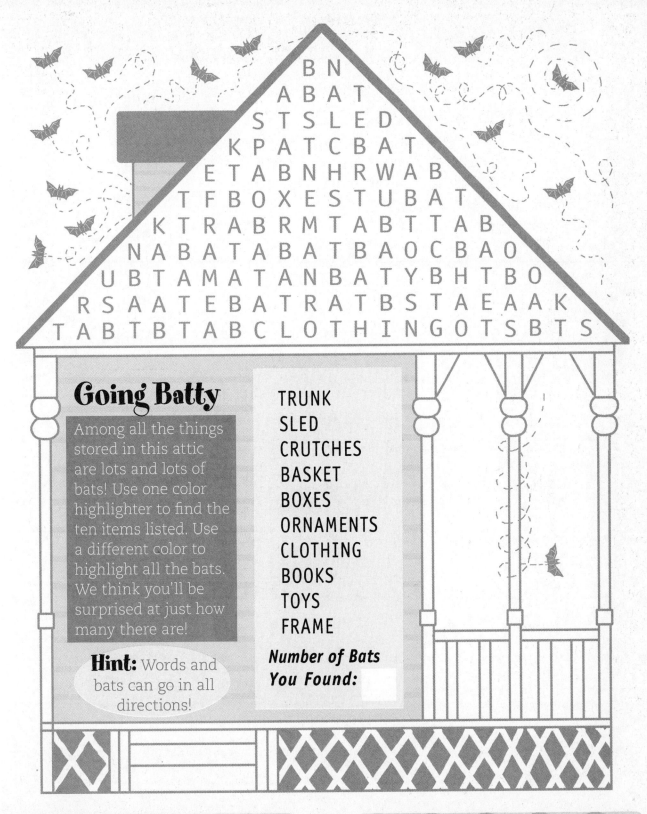

```
B N
A B A T
S T S L E D
K P A T C B A T
E T A B N H R W A B
T F B O X E S T U B A T
K T R A B R M T A B T T A B
N A B A T A B A T B A O C B A O
U B T A M A T A N B A T Y B H T B O
R S A A T E B A T R A T B S T A E A A K
T A B T B T A B C L O T H I N G O T S B T S
```

# Going Batty

Among all the things stored in this attic are lots and lots of bats! Use one color highlighter to find the ten items listed. Use a different color to highlight all the bats. We think you'll be surprised at just how many there are!

**Hint:** Words and bats can go in all directions!

TRUNK
SLED
CRUTCHES
BASKET
BOXES
ORNAMENTS
CLOTHING
BOOKS
TOYS
FRAME

*Number of Bats
You Found:*

TRASH BAG

RUBBER GLOVES

SPONGE

# More Chores!

Helping around the house seems like endless work. Just when you finish one task, there is something else to do—sort of like this puzzle! You must find a string of words one right after the other. The trick is that the last letter of each word is the first letter of the next one!

We left you the first word of the string, and a jumbled list of all the other words. Put them in order, and good luck with your chores!

1 vacuum
_ weeds
_ tidy
_ mow
_ polished
_ scrub
_ helps
_ sweep
_ dust
_ brush

```
D R U B B E R G L O V E S
U O N V C E U P O N A D C
S T T R A S H B A G E I R
T M E T H C R E R E E W U
P E E W S O U A W S A P B
A O R I O P N U O C E R S
N N L M A M L E M D U A E
T P A I L B E E T S H G G
O O H N S P E R H B Y E N
B M Y S A H T F R I D E O
N G D O J E E N N Y I L P
I V S E D N E D U S T X S
```

**Extra Fun:** After you've found the entire word string, try to find the names of the eight cleaning supplies you see listed around the page.

# Fun for Frank

On a rainy day, Frank likes to read a book, use his computer, or watch TV. Find eight words related to each activity in the three mini word searches. The trick is to figure out which puzzle grid each word is in!

# Movie Night

You're having some friends sleep over—which films might you watch? See what's available by matching the two halves of each movie title. Then highlight these films in the letter grid! Careful: Four of the films have titles that are only one word.

**Extra Fun:** Find six food items kids love to munch on while watching movies!

Bedknobs
Charlotte's
Chicken
Finding
Freaky
Ghost
Happy
Lion
Little
Madagascar
Mary
Pinocchio
Star
Wizard

Poppins
Aladdin
busters
Cars
Feet
Friday
King
Mermaid
Nemo
of Oz
and Broomsticks
Run
Web
Wars

```
G M Y A L I T T L E M E R M A I D L L T I M P E
H A P P Y F E E T I F A V O A R I T E M O V O C
O I E I I R S T H R O E O R I R G I C A R S P H
S N A N L E V P E A R N S C I O Y N O F T H C A
T E L O R A O I D C U C K H E R S P W I T H O R
B Z A C R K O Z M S O S W I Z A R D O F O Z R L
U T D C L Y A Z N A D G E C N N E W I P L D N O
S E D H M F Y A N G E C X K T G F C H I P S A T
T V I I R R I T E A M A O E V I E I S T H I E T
E O N O I I F I N D I N G N E M O G I N S A N E
R L P R I D E A N A D D P R R E J U D I O C E S
S T A R W A R S W M I Y T U H S I R L A D U R W
E N C E O Y L I V I E R A N I C E C R E A M N E
B E D K N O B S A N D B R O O M S T I C K S D B
```

## Monday

```
C H I B L Y H
F A I R I C O
S T E E R O S
W S S E A O U
T W Y Z N L Y
E R E Y I I N
D R W R M D N
```

## Tuesday

```
I C L O U D Y
S H O W E R S
W I R A N I I
A L W T E Z W
R L E O L Z N
N Y L V E L D
R N Y A I E Y
```

COOL     BREEZY     CLOUDY

FAIR

DRY

### Five-Day Forecast

Twenty weather words are scattered across these pages. All of them can be found in the small grids. When you have located four words for each day, you will know what the weather will be this week!

BRIGHT

DRIZZLE

CHILLY     HAZY     HOT

## Wednesday

| | | | | | | |
|---|---|---|---|---|---|---|
| A | C | P | H | Z | Y | L |
| U | O | O | W | A | R | N |
| D | Y | U | N | W | E | T |
| M | I | R | A | I | N | Y |
| L | G | I | H | N | T | W |
| D | I | N | T | D | H | S |
| T | A | G | R | Y | S | A |

## Thursday

| | | | | | | |
|---|---|---|---|---|---|---|
| A | B | R | O | W | R | H |
| U | R | N | D | A | O | T |
| M | I | L | D | M | I | Y |
| T | G | W | H | R | N | O |
| W | H | Y | A | N | R | H |
| E | T | E | U | M | Y | T |
| W | S | S | W | A | R | M |

## Friday

| | | | | | | |
|---|---|---|---|---|---|---|
| B | O | R | W | R | M | I |
| R | H | A | Z | Y | S | C |
| G | U | O | I | K | P | L |
| T | M | T | T | C | O | D |
| M | I | R | A | I | U | Y |
| O | D | M | E | T | N | I |
| H | T | O | C | S | G | A |

HUMID

MILD

SUNNY

SHOWERS

STICKY

POURING

WARM

# Backyard Birds

Listed below are two dozen common backyard birds in alphabetical order. You should be able to find all of them in the feeder. Be careful, though, because four of the bird names have been scrambled. You'll have to figure out which bird to look for before you can find it in the grid!

BLUEBIRD

BLUE JAY

BUNTING

DINRACDAL

CHICKADEE

CROW

FLICKER

GOLDFINCH

GROSBEAK

KAWH

JUNCO

MARTIN

MOURNING DOVE

NUTHATCH

ORIOLE

PHOEBE

BRONI

SPARROW

SWIFT

TITMOUSE

VIREO

WARBLER

REPODWOECK

WREN

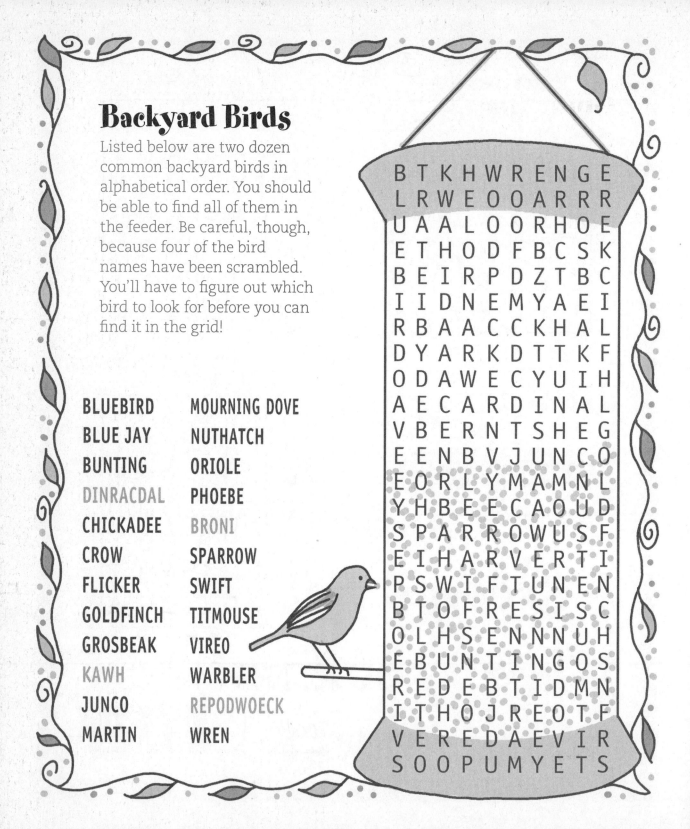

```
B T K H W R E N G E
L R W E O O A R R R
U A A L O O R H O E
E T H O D F B C S K
B E I R P D Z T B C
I I D N E M Y A E I
R B A A C C K H A L
D Y A R K D T T K F
O D A W E C Y U I H
A E C A R D I N A L
V B E R N T S H E G
E E N B V J U N C O
E O R L Y M A M N L
Y H B E E C A O U D
S P A R R O W U S F
E I H A R V E R T I
P S W I F T U N E N
B T O F R E S I S C
O L H S E N N N U H
E B U N T I N G O S
R E D E B T I D M N
I T H O J R E O T F
V E R E D A E V I R
S O O P U M Y E T S
```

# Going Buggy

Find all fifteen insects hidden in the grid. Read the remaining letters from left to right and top to bottom to reveal a silly bug joke and its answer!

Remember to look for bugs up, down, sideways, backwards, and diagonally.

ANT
BEE
FLEA
FLY
TICK
GNAT
SPIDER

BEETLE
TERMITE
BUTTERFLY
COCKROACH
DRAGONFLY
FIREFLY
LADYBUG
MOSQUITO

```
W K C I T H Y D O
B E O E E E B G S
B U C Z F Z U R ?
O B K E L B T E C
T A R U Y E T D E
I S O D E E E I T
U T A H E T R P I
Q L C Y C L F S M
S T H A A E L F R
O G N A T N Y T E
M W H A I S T L T
D R A G O N F L Y
E Y L F E R I F !
```

# Obstacle Course Opposites

GO      OVER
UP      FIRST
IN      LONG
HIGH   SLOW
PUSH   FORWARD

↻ Look for the OPPOSITE of these words!

Oliver has set up an amazing obstacle course in his yard. Think of the opposite word for the ten words listed. Find the new words in the grid.

**Hint:** The words can go across the dotted lines!

# Great Gardens

Mom and Dad are out working in the yard. Search among the W-E-E-Ds for the nine varieties of plants hidden in each garden.

**Hint:** Mom loves flowers and Dad is crazy about vegetables.

CARROT        LETTUCE        POTATO        VIOLET
CORN          MARIGOLD       ROSE          ZUCCHINI
CUCUMBER      MUM            TOMATO
DAISY         PANSY          TULIP
EGGPLANT      PEPPER
GERANIUM      PETUNIA

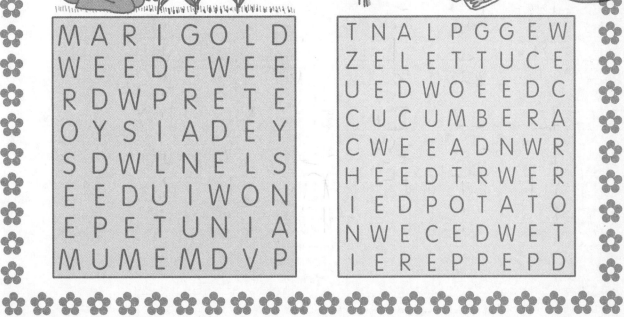

```
M A R I G O L D
W E E D E W E E
R D W P R E T E
O Y S I A D E Y
S D W L N E L S
E E D U I W O N
E P E T U N I A
M U M E M D V P
```

```
T N A L P G G E W
Z E L E T T U C E
U E D W O E E D C
C U C U M B E R A
C W E E A D N W R
H E E D T R W E R
I E D P O T A T O
N W E C E D W E T
I E R E P P E P D
```

# Fantastic Fort

Some great forts for kids have been built in trees! In this puzzle, you will look for trees and shrubs, tree parts, and tools used to build a tree fort. Use a light marker to highlight all these words in the letter grid. Then use the same color marker to highlight the extra letter Fs.

ASH       DARK      STUMP     POPLAR
ELM       ROOT      SUMAC     WILLOW
FIR       PINE      SPRUCE    HICKORY
IVY       BEECH     BALSAM    JUNIPER
OAK       LILAC     HAMMER    REDWOOD
SAW       MAPLE     LADDER    SYCAMORE
YEW       NAILS     LAUREL    WISTERIA
BUD       OLIVE     BAMBOO    CRABAPPLE
LEAF      TRUNK     BRANCH    HYDRANGEA
PALM      BIRCH     CHESTNUT  HONEYSUCKLE
TWIG      HOLLY     DOGWOOD   COTTONWOOD

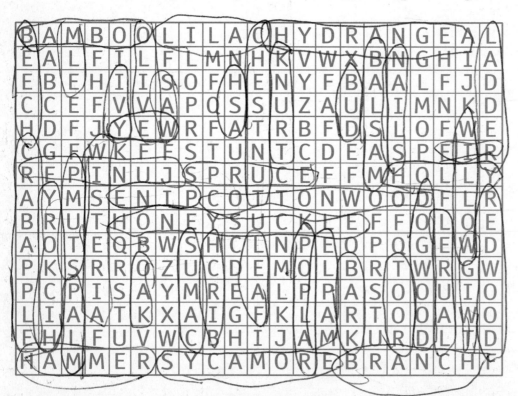

## More Fun

Use a dark colored marker to color in the squares with the remaining letters. You will see that someone has put a silly message on this fort!

20

# Ready to Ride

Before you hop on your bike, see if you can find all fifteen bicycle parts hidden in the wheels.

BRAKE ~~BRAKE~~  RIM ~~RIM~~
CHAIN ~~CHAIN~~  SEAT ~~SEAT~~
FRAME ~~FRAME~~  SPOKE ~~SPOKE~~
GEAR ~~GEAR~~  TOECLIP ~~TOECLIP~~
TIRE ~~TIRE~~  WHEEL ~~WHEEL~~
LEVER ~~LEVER~~  REFLECTOR ~~REFLECTOR~~
PEDAL ~~PEDAL~~  HANDLEBARS ~~HANDLEBARS~~
RACK ~~RACK~~

B R G E
O M W E O I
T P C H A I N K
O B S T E R K E D B
U R E E E R M L L R
H A N D L E B A R S
S K H A N D L D E K
E I C H A N E N
E K O P S P
W E E L

H T N U
K C R I F O
H T H O H R I M
R A O A T C A E U S
B N E I C U M U H B
K D C L E V E R A K R
E L L I B L S R A N R
B I A F P I C D
P S E A T K
N R A B

21

## Outdoor Eating

It's time for a barbecue! What items often get cooked on the grill, and what foods do people expect on the picnic table? These items are so familiar that there's no list of words, but here is a hint: There are twenty foods in all.

Don't forget that words can go in all directions, and diagonally too!

# Hide & Seek

Use the alphabet-to-number decoder at the bottom of the page to figure out the outdoor hiding spots we've hidden in the grid.

12-7-7-3-10

11-9-4-4

10-6-4-3

8-7-9-2-6

| 12 | 7 | 10 | 6 | 4 | 4 | 5 | 8 |
|----|---|----|---|---|---|---|---|
| 7 | 12 | 7 | 7 | 3 | 10 | 1 | 7 |
| 1 | 7 | 2 | 9 | 8 | 6 | 3 | 9 |
| 3 | 1 | 10 | 3 | 3 | 4 | 2 | 2 |
| 11 | 9 | 4 | 4 | 11 | 3 | 4 | 6 |
| 5 | 1 | 6 | 5 | 2 | 12 | 7 | 7 |
| 6 | 3 | 5 | 1 | 9 | 1 | 5 | 4 |

1=A
2=C
3=D
4=E
5=G
6=H
7=O
8=P
9=R
10=S
11=T
12=W

# Driveway Fun

The kids have been having a grand time playing outside. See if you can find all of their toys hidden in the driveway grid.

car     hula hoop
bat     jumprope
bike    balloon
ball    truck
chalk
jacks

```
                    A
                   B A T
                  H A I C D
                 E U I L K E T
                T T L O L A E L D
               I K R A A S T O R E O
              K R O U H A E T A P Y P T
             E S A B C O N L O N O U R D
            B B U M M E O R B U Y A U N
           A J U M P R O P E R N A C S
          I A L B I K O W T R A N K E
         T C R A B L O C A T C M C H
        A K A P P L L E K G S E I N
       A S I R I A E T S E O R T A
      O C H N I B E S S O T N S N
     S E D A L B R E L L O R
    D S B E E S T W G H
   E B A L L O O N
    O Q L I P A
     U T S K
      K Y
```

pogostick

rollerblades

skateboard

kite    rocket

ramp    bubbles

yoyo    wagon    marbles

Chapter 3

# At School

**AISLE, CHILDREN, DOOR, DRIVER, ENGINE, FLOOR, HORN, MIRRORS, SEATS, STOP SIGN, WHEELS, WINDOWS, WINDSHIELD, WIPERS**

# Hop on the Bus

Every day, the school bus picks up children all around town. Use a yellow marker to highlight these fourteen familiar things you would find on a school bus.

# School Stuff

We bet you know your way around a school! Match a word from column 1 with a word from column 2. Find both words together in the grid.

Column 1:

CLASS
PRINCIPAL'S
WATER
LIBRARY
FLAG
CHALK
HALL
BUS

Column 2:

FOUNTAIN
BOARD
ROOM
BOOK
STOP
OFFICE
POLE
WAY

```
P R I N C I P A L S O F F I C E
S A C P L E S C H O L O L Y O L
T B H Q A D R A O B K L A H C I
E C A L S K B R D E X W G I E B
P O T S S U B I F F L G P H I A
B C D E R F R O O L M L O O R R
A R K O O B Y R A R B I L F J Y
S U S T O L I H O M N O E F K B
C L A S M W A T R F O N T O N O
W A T E R F O U N T A I N E X K
```

# Plenty of Pals

```
X P U P P Y I P P I P D P A T R I C K G
P R I S C I L L A B C H E F P E N C I L
H P I Z Z A A P P U F F Y H I P A N S Y
I P L A Y P A U L P A R T L P I L L C W
L P X P O M P P         L J K R P E
O A A X E B E A         L I E M I C
M B Y L A G N I         N P S A R N
E E A X M C G L         E O P L A E
N B P O T E D Y P O N C H O R P Q U T D
A E X P A T R I C I A P I N T S E A E U
P O T E P P E N G U I N T Y L L O P U R
I H T R O P H I L L I P P U D D L E V P
G P O S P P P A
P P C E C I I I
A O S P O C N T
T T E H R K O R
I A R O N R L O
E T P N D I P P
N O F E G H E J
C C P P E T T K
E D P A R K E R
E S P A R K R P
L A C S A P M O
P E Y C R E P O
O N N O G N P D
R I P I Q N A L
T H A R S Y N E
S P I E R R E T
```

Pippi knows thirty kids at school whose names all start with the letter P! Can you find all of Pippi's pals in the grid?

## Extra Fun:

— Could any of the names be given to either a boy or a girl?

— Which name is hidden twice?

— While you are looking for names in the grid, what else do you notice about this puzzle?

Hi, Polly, Peter, and Penelope!

Hi, Pippi!

**Paige**
**Palmer**
**Pamela**
**Pansy**
**Parker**
**Pascal**
**Patience**
**Patricia**
**Patrick**
**Paul**
**Paula**
**Pedro**
**Peggy**
**Penny**
**Pepe**
**Percy**
**Persephone**
**Peter**
**Phillip**
**Philomena**
**Phineas**
**Phoebe**
**Phyllis**
**Pierre**
**Pippi**
**Polly**
**Portia**
**Prescott**
**Priscilla**
**Prudence**

# What's in the Backpack?

You can learn a lot about kids from their backpacks! Find all the words and you will know Stacey and Tracey's favorite subjects—and school supplies!

ART, BINDER, COMPUTER, ENGLISH, ERASER, FOLDER, GYM, HISTORY, LUNCH, MARKER, MATH, MUSIC, PAPER, PEN, PENCIL, READING, RULER, SCIENCE

**STACEY**

```
Y R O T S I H
K E R A R B A
N P E N C I L
E A A B T N U
P P D R C D N
M E I D T E C
U R N E F R H
S G G Y M H I
H S I L G N E
```

**TRACEY**

```
R F O L D E R
E R U L E S J
T M U S I C K
U A L P E I R
P R M A R E U
M K M M S N L
O E O A P C E
C R R T Q E R
P E T H M A T
```

# Shape Up!

Fifteen words related to shapes are scattered around this page. The trick is to figure out whether they belong in the circle, the triangle, or the square!

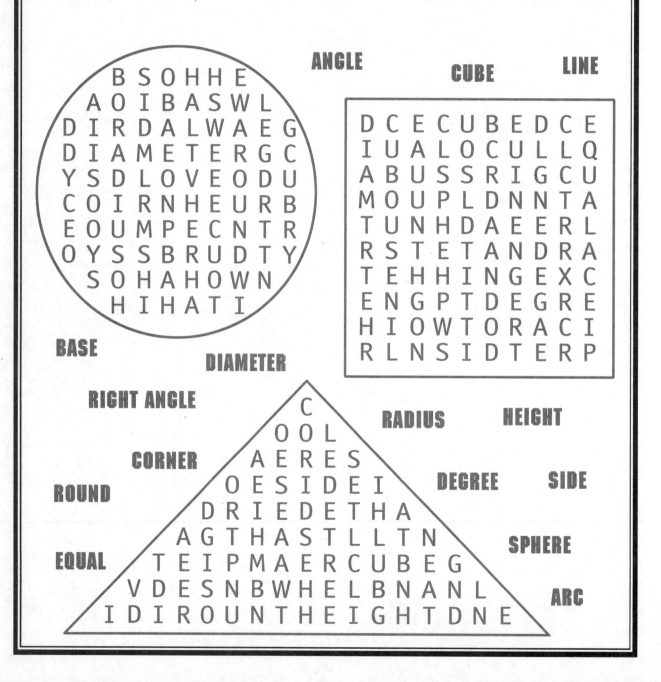

**ANGLE**    **CUBE**    **LINE**

B S O H H E
A O I B A S W L
D I R D A L W A E G
D I A M E T E R G C
Y S D L O V E O D U
C O I R N H E U R B
E O U M P E C N T R
O Y S S B R U D T Y
S O H A H O W N
H I H A T I

D C E C U B E D C E
I U A L O C U L L Q
A B U S S R I G C U
M O U P L D N N T A
T U N H D A E E R L
R S T E T A N D R A
T E H H I N G E X C
E N G P T D E G R E
H I O W T O R A C I
R L N S I D T E R P

**BASE**

**DIAMETER**

**RIGHT ANGLE**

**CORNER**

**ROUND**

**EQUAL**

**RADIUS**    **HEIGHT**

**DEGREE**    **SIDE**

**SPHERE**

**ARC**

C
O O L
A E R E S
O E S I D E I
D R I E D E T H A
A G T H A S T L L T N
T E I P M A E R C U B E G
V D E S N B W H E L B N A N L
I D I R O U N T H E I G H T D N E

# You're It!

It's a game of tag at recess! Move quickly through the letters picking up eight "fast" words as you go. Rules: Words follow one after the other in an unbroken line. Move up, down, and sideways, but not diagonally. Words can spell around corners!

1. **CHASE**   2. **SPRINT**   3. **DASH**   4. **RUN**

5. **QUICK**   6. **HUSTLE**   7. **SWIFT**   8. **SPEED**

START

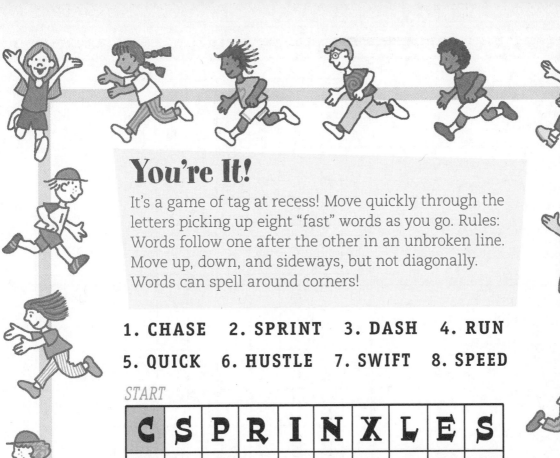

| C | S | P | R | I | N | X | L | E | S |
|---|---|---|---|---|---|---|---|---|---|
| H | E | R | I | K | Y | S | T | O | W |
| A | S | I | N | I | L | U | S | F | I |
| S | H | S | T | L | K | H | U | T | S |
| E | R | A | D | O | C | K | P | E | P |
| S | U | N | Q | U | I | C | K | E | D |

END

# Got Art?

Follow the directions to see what Maya is painting in art class. Find the six words and fill in their boxes with the colors suggested.

Blue: PAINT, WATER, EASEL, SMOCK

Green: PAINTBRUSH, PAPER

Then fill in the boxes Y, B, and G using this color chart:

Y = YELLOW

B = BLUE

G = GREEN

| F | J | R | U | K | B | S | I | T | E | L |
|---|---|---|---|---|---|---|---|---|---|---|
| A | B | B | F | B | B | B | C | B | B | X |
| V | B | B | B | C | B | E | B | B | B | M |
| K | Z | B | P | A | I | N | T | S | J | C |
| X | B | C | E | B | Y | B | S | F | B | W |
| B | B | B | A | Y | Y | Y | M | B | B | B |
| L | B | F | S | B | Y | B | O | F | B | M |
| F | E | R | E | T | A | W | C | B | E | I |
| C | B | B | L | O | H | P | K | B | B | H |
| N | B | B | D | E | S | O | Q | B | B | P |
| A | C | T | F | R | U | H | S | M | O | A |
| E | W | N | E | S | R | U | M | D | F | I |
| A | F | A | A | M | B | H | E | A | S | T |
| P | G | W | S | C | T | R | S | H | G | E |
| A | G | G | F | K | N | U | X | G | G | A |
| N | G | G | G | X | I | S | G | G | G | S |
| T | R | G | G | G | A | G | G | G | X | L |
| W | A | T | P | A | P | E | R | H | R | U |

# Janitor's Closet

You never know what Jack the Janitor will have in his closet. Can you find all twenty-five items?

```
T H I S C L D O S E
P B A N D A I D S H
A C L E A N S E R S
P T U X I S I T O I
E T N T A L N L Y L
R F C E U T F P L O
T S H N L R E O O P
O E B S V A C U U M
W V O I F S T A L F
E O X O L H A K S L
L L I N T B N T A A
L G L C O A T D O S
S I O O I G O F O S H
T U G R L S S B L
R E E H D E F U A I
E T T H T I N T G G
V I S B P P I W T H
I R S U H A M M E R T
R D H L O P T I R H S
D W A B T E E D I Y T
W E H S O R K I E S C
E R A G S L C K S O S
R C E T A T U M Y H O
S H A T U B R O O M
```

BANDAIDS
BATTERIES
BOOTS
BROOM
BUCKET
CLEANSERS
COAT
DISINFECTANT
EXTENSION CORD
FLASHLIGHT
GLOVES
HAMMER
HAT
KEYS
LIGHTBULBS
LUNCHBOX
MOP
PAPER TOWELS
PHOTOS
POLISH
RAGS
SCREWDRIVER
TOILET PAPER
TRASHBAGS
VACUUM

# Lunch Line

Something weird has happened to the menu in the school cafeteria! Solve the simple first-to-last code, and then find the five food items each student has picked to eat. All items are used at least once, but some are used twice!

Try using a single line of color to highlight each word as you find it!

IZZAP     OUPS

OTDOGH     ALADS

ANDWICHS     RIESF

I P U O S T H I
N K T H A E T C
S A N D W I C H
I L I K E K L I
U D D U L O A P
N C H I B O P S
E S M T O C P F

A I L C O R N
T Z H H E M E
C Z A I L S E
J U I C E B L
O E C K A U P
O S P E A S P
K E U N S E A

# Detention!

There are many reasons you might have to stay after school for detention. Highlight these thirteen reasons in the grid, and then gather the leftover letters from left to right and top to bottom. Write them in order on the dotted lines to reveal a silly joke and its silly answer!

___ ___ ___ _____

_____ _____?

__ ___ _ _____

_____!

**DISRESPECTFUL**
**FIGHT**
**HITTING**
**KICK**
**LYING**
**RUDE**
**SPITTING**
**STEAL**
**SWEAR**
**TARDINESS**
**THREAT**
**VANDALISM**
**VIOLENCE**

```
D I S R E S P E C T F U L
E W T H U Y T G W A S T S
C H E E M D A N A L G N W
N E A T G I E I V Y E N E
E D L E T E R T N I T I A
L O N F I G H T ? N H E R
O H A H I T T I N G D K A
I N E G A T I P V E A C T
V A N D A L I S M T I I T
U T A R D I N E S S D K E
```

# Chapter 4
# In the Community

# Around Town

Fill in the blanks in each of these sentences about your community. Find each of the places or people in the letter grid on the next page!

1. Visit the _ _ _ _ _ _ _ _ when you need a good book.

2. Call the _ _ _ _ _ _ to report a crime!

3. Your dog gets its shots at the _ _ _ .

4. Fill the fridge at the _ _ _ _ _ _ _ _  _ _ _ _ _ _ .

5. On Sunday, you might go to _ _ _ _ _ _ _ with your family.

6. By some stamps and mail a letter at the
_ _ _ _  _ _ _ _ _ _ _ .

7. Mom will call the _ _ _ _ _ _ _ if you feel sick.

8. Pick up a hammer and some nails at the
_ _ _ _ _ _ _ _ _  _ _ _ _ _ .

9. The _ _ _ _ _ is the place to have a savings account.

10. If you need a haircut, visit a _ _ _ _ _ _ _ _ _ _ _ _ .

11. See a matinee at the _ _ _ _ _ _  _ _ _ _ _ _ _ _ .

12. The _ _ _ _ _ _ _ _ _ _ _ _ _ _ will respond if a building is burning!

38

```
B F A N K I W I H A I D R E
S I M O V I E T H E A T E R
G R O C E R Y S T O R E H O
R E S S E R D R I A H I C T
O F D R S S R U P O L C E S
D I F H A R D V I N D C S E
A G D R A W I M E N B H S R
E H Y G A L K O R T A U E A
C T E R A N D V Y D N R R W
I E O N A E F I R O T C O D
L R O B R R E T T H I H S R
O S W A R E B H P F I R F A
P O S T O F F I C E U Z Z H
E S O I D I D N L T H A V E
```

# Savings Sum

Ethan has been saving coins. Now he wants to deposit the money at the bank! Find all the PENNIES, NICKELS, DIMES, and QUARTERS in the letter grid, and then add them up to see how much money Ethan has saved. Clue: The piggy bank is really full!

# Love Letter

Scott is at the post office to mail a valentine to a special friend. What does the card say? Start at the white letter and read all the way around the edge of the valentine to find the first seven words of a familiar verse. Now look for the remaining six words in the center of the heart!

**Extra Fun:** See how many "kisses" Scott included on his card!

R _ _ _ _ _

A _ _

R _ _.

V _ _ _ _ _ _

A _ _

B _ _ _.

S _ _ _ _ _

I _

S _ _ _ _ _,

A _ _

S _

A _ _

Y _ _!

# In the Bag

What did Mom buy at the grocery store? Look for the sixteen food items in the grocery bags. Which item isn't there? **Hint:** The words are separated into the bags by type of food!

BANANA, BEANS, BREAD, BUTTER, CARROT, CEREAL, CHEESE, COOKIES, EGGS, LETTUCE, MILK, NUTS, PASTA, PLUM, SOUP, YOGURT

```
B A N A N A I
E C U T T E L
A C O M O O K
N E U I R S B
S L I L R H U
P O P O A E T
M G G K C Y R
```

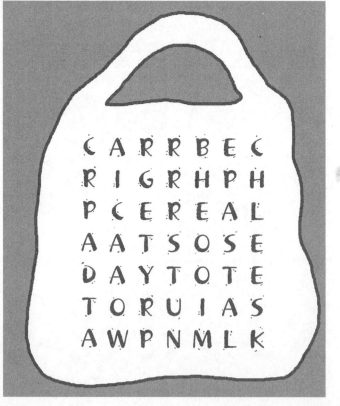

```
D C E S O O P
Y O G U R T E
A H G D E D S
M E S Y T N E
O I I S T U E
A E L L U S H
B R E K B T C
```

```
C A R R B E C
R I G R H P H
P C E R E A L
A A T S O S E
D A Y T O T E
T O R U I A S
A W P N M L K
```

# Snip! Snip!

When your hair gets shaggy, it's time to visit the barber. Let's give these words a haircut! Remove one letter from each to make a new word. The ten new words are the ones you will find in the grid—they are all in different places! Extra Fun: Some of the words can be "trimmed" twice to make two new words.

```
S A H U L E M A
R B A R I A B O
A J K H E R I M
E B N B J S A B
H A I R B A Q L
E L Q F H I L I
B O C R B N I P
```

**SHEARS** becomes _ _ _ _ _ _ and _ _ _ _ _

**CHAIR** becomes _ _ _ _ _ and _ _ _ _

**SINK** becomes _ _ _ _ and _ _ _

**SNIP** becomes _ _ _ _

**COMB** becomes _ _ _

**TRIM** becomes _ _ _ _

**CLIP** becomes _ _ _

# On Fire!

Things sure are hot around here! Use the definitions to figure out all the words that have F-I-R-E in them. Look for these words in the letter grid on the next page. Extra Fun: In the puzzle, the letters F-I-R-E look like a bunch of flames!

Where Christmas stockings are hung = __ __ __ __ __ __ __ __ __

Small beetle that gives off light = __ __ __ __ __ __ __ __

An uncontrolled blaze in the woods = __ __ __ __ __ __ __ __ __ __

A small explosive lit on holidays = __ __ __ __ __ __ __ __ __ __ __ __

Building for "pumper trucks" = __ __ __ __ __ __ __ __ __ __

Cannot be damaged by burning = __ __ __ __ __ __ __ __ __ __ __

What you burn in a fireplace = __ __ __ __ __ __ __ __ __

A place where you toast marshmallows = __ __ __ __ __ __ __ __ __ __

Long red truck with a loud siren = __ __ __ __ __   __ __ __ __ __ __ __

Explosive noise from an engine = __ __ __ __ __ __ __ __ __

Device that sprays foam on flames =

__ __ __ __   __ __ __ __ __ __ __ __ __ __ __

Colorful display on the 4th of July = __ __ __ __ __ __ __ __ __ __ __

Person who puts out a burning house =

__ __ __ __ __ __ __ __ __ __ __ __

I T C A M P 🔥 R L M H I
W N K T H A E H 🔥 S E F
I 🔥 T T H K X S Y N E O
L P R E C I T S I N O O
D L T A 🔥 F I G H T E R
🔥 A R H I N N G N I S P
R C C E R E G T H A U 🔥
🔥 E S I 🔥 T U 🔥 W O O D
K T I N G B I Y A C H A
C M P Y F I S H L Y 🔥 R
A E T L O A H L 🔥 N H B
B M N F S T E T R Q 🔥 C
Q 🔥 Z 🔥 W O R K S R N T

# Handy Hardware

Search the local hardware store for sixteen items you might need for that next home-improvement project!

HOSE, LAWNMOWER, PAINT, SHOVEL, RAKE, PAIL, NAILS, BROOM, SEEDS, BATTERY, WHEELBARROW, ROPE, SAND, SHADE, SPONGE, DOORKNOB

```
E E D I R E W O M N W A L
U S O P A I B W E A D Y I
S P O N G E R H T I O R A
H L R O S H O V E L V E P
A D K E E B O E K S P T B
D E N T E A M E A O G T A
E S O A D T O L R T O A R
H O B T S P A I N T H B R
W H E E L B A R R O W E O
```

Chapter 5

# On Vacation

# Road Trip

There are always lots of things to pack for a road trip. Look in the little car to find all the items pictured here. Do you think they will all fit?

**Helpful Hint:** The pictures may bring to mind several different words. For example, you might look for "puppy" when the word we've hidden is "dog." Keep looking until you find the correct word for each picture!

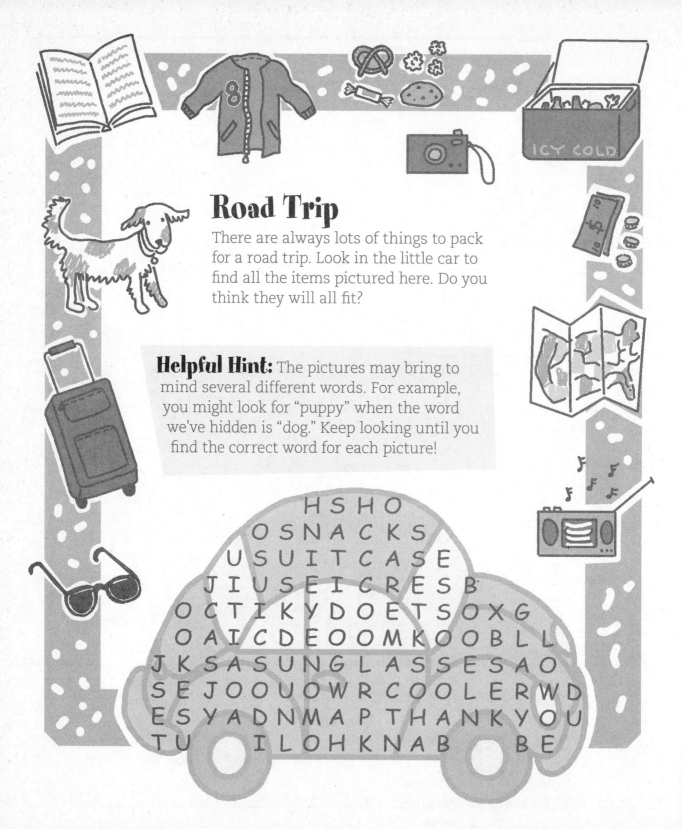

```
        H S H O
      O S N A C K S
      U S U I T C A S E
      J I U S E I C R E S B
    O C T I K Y D O E T S O X G
    O A I C D E O O M K O O B L L
  J K S A S U N G L A S S E S A O
  S E J O O U O W R C O O L E R W D
  E S Y A D N M A P T H A N K Y O U
  T U   I L O H K N A B     B E
```

# New Hampshire Holiday

Driving through scenic New Hampshire, you can learn a lot from a map! Find all twenty words listed here, but also look for one other place of interest that is plentiful in this state. How many times do you find it in the grid?

AIRPORT, BORDER, CAMPSITE, CITIES, COVERED BRIDGE, ELEVATION, EXITS, FOREST, GOLF COURSE, HIGHWAY, HOSPITAL, LAKE, MILES, MOUNTAIN, PICNIC AREA, RIVER, ROADS, SKI AREA, TOLL, TOWN

```
X L R T R O P R I A R P A R K H
E L E V A T I O N E E T O W N I
T X V P A R K F R R D E P H T G
I M I L E S S K I A R E A O S H
S E R T E G O L F C O U R S E W
P O R I S P R A P I B D K P R A
M I T D P A R K E N T H E I O Y
A I A P A R K E G C L L O T F G
C O V E R E D B R I D G E A R A
R N I A T N U O M P A R K L N I
```

# Motor Messages

On a cross-country trip, you will see lots of silly sayings on license plates. Even the spelling is silly! Figure out the real message on each of these license plates, and then look for it spelled out in the grid.

| | | |
|---|---|---|
| BCNU | GR82CU | I12BUGU |
| 2DUM2NO | UR1DRFL | W84ME |
| CRAZ4U | LUV2LAF | ZPDDUDA |

```
N L O Z I S L A R O F E M I T E H T R
Y O U A R E W O N D E R F U L T H Z W
G V O O D M E N T O C O M E T O A I H
O E D I W A N T T O B U G Y O U O G O
H T F T H E I R P A R T Y I B E L R L
D O I E B E S E E I N G Y O U V E E E
E L T H I S S I T H E T S E B R A A N
W A I T F O R M E N D O M U O H T T U
A U G H T O T A R E N E G R I N T T B
R G H E W O T O O D U M B T O K N O W
I H R L D L Z Z U P S I H T E K I S C
F M I W O N D E R W O H J E N Z L E H
Z I P P I T Y D O O D A H Y W I L E O
O L L I N N A E N E R I T C O L U Y L
R G O T T O F I C R A Z Y F O R Y O U
E H T O N A T O O R R F I T A R D U T
```

50

# Under the Big Top

Vacation is a great time to see the circus! Find the words hidden in the three rings. When you are done, you will know what act is performing in each place. Careful—one piece of equipment is not used!

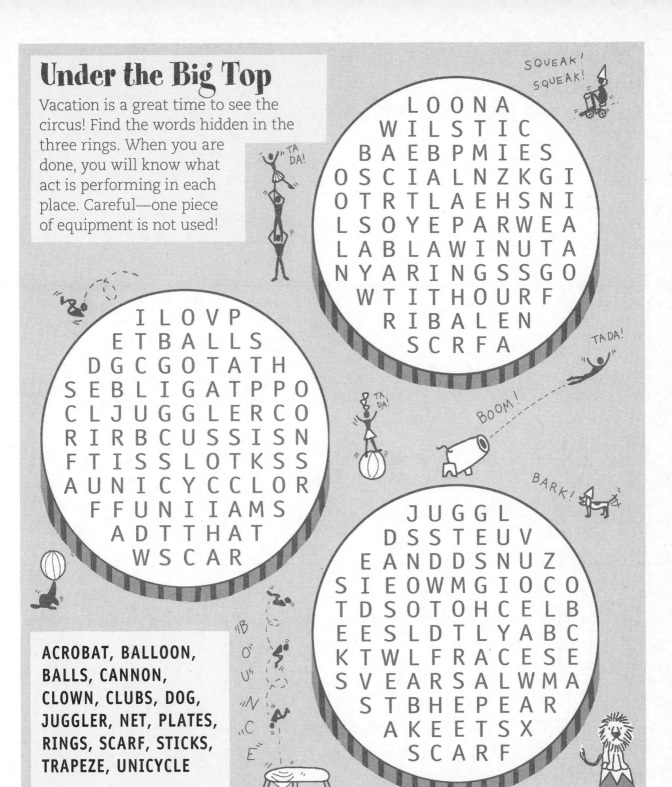

**ACROBAT, BALLOON, BALLS, CANNON, CLOWN, CLUBS, DOG, JUGGLER, NET, PLATES, RINGS, SCARF, STICKS, TRAPEZE, UNICYCLE**

# Gearing Up

It is important to take the right equipment if you plan to go camping on your vacation. See if you can find all ten items hiding in the grassy field!

**BACKPACK**
**BINOCULARS**
**CANTEEN**
**COOLER**
**FIRST AID KIT**
**HIKING BOOTS**
**LANTERN**
**MATCHES**
**SLEEPING BAG**
**TENT**

```
I L B A C K S S T O O B G N I K I H
K A E O O U A E B I N O S E D T O L
B N E T V E I H T H I K N G O C O C
O T P M E P D C I N B A C K P A C K
O E I B E N K T G F O O R B A N L I
S R F I R S T A I D K I T I E T A P
T N N E T I C M K S C A B N M E N P
S R A L U C O N I B C C O O L E R I
B O C K P O C K R A W L O D A N L C
O S L E E P I N G B A G T B O O H K
```

# Sunny Seashore

Building at the beach is great fun! Find ten items used to make sandcastles. Then use a dark marker to put a large dot of color over all the letters D-I-G that are not part of the answer words. Connect the dots to make block letters that spell out one more item you really need at the beach!

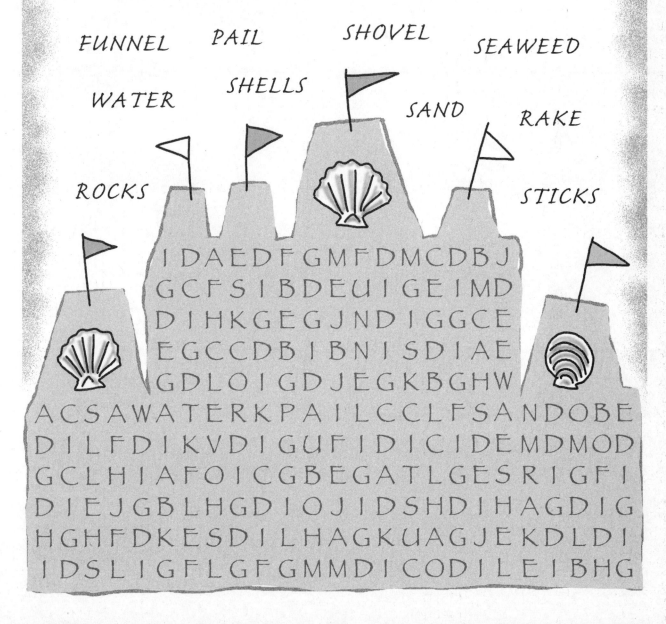

FUNNEL     PAIL     SHOVEL     SEAWEED

WATER     SHELLS          SAND     RAKE

ROCKS                              STICKS

```
I D A E D F G M F D M C D B J
G C F S I B D E U I G E I M D
D I H K G E G J N D I G G C E
E G C C D B I B N I S D I A E
G D L O I G D J E G K B G H W
A C S A W A T E R K P A I L C C L F S A N D O B E
D I L F D I K V D I G U F I D I C I D E M D M O D
G C L H I A F O I C G B E G A T L G E S R I G F I
D I E J G B L H G D I O J I D S H D I H A G D I G
H G H F D K E S D I L H A G K U A G J E K D L D I
I D S L I G F L G F G M M D I C O D I L E I B H G
```

# Sail Away

A sailing trip would be a great vacation! Find fifteen parts of a sailboat hidden in the sail.

```
        R
      R I
      I E G
      J K L G
      C E L I
      E A E I N
      D P P L T G
      S A N C H O R
      J Y H U L L D E
      A T B I R R T H D
      P S T A R B O A R D
      A A R Y A I O U M U
      M E B O W R J I O D R
      X A M A P S T E R N M C
```

ANCHOR, BOOM, BOW, DECK, HULL, JIB, KEEL, MAST, PORT, RIGGING, RUDDER, SHROUD, STARBOARD, STERN, TILLER

# What a Zoo!

The zoo animals are on vacation, running loose! In which exhibit does each belong?

TOUCAN  EMU

ANACONDA

WALLABY

LION

SLOTH

GIRAFFE

RHINOCEROS

WOMBAT

```
O H J M Y G A O D
A N A C O N D A N
E S G S I A T H I
N K U I W C I L L
O R A N G U T A N
S T R O N O G L E
M Y S L O T H S E
```
**South American Exhibit**

```
I T K H M Y O W
N B O R Y A S S
I W O M B A T E
R E K B A L A B
O R A A L X O O
L A B B L L E O
O O U G A N M K
X I R D W C U A
O O R A G N A K
T R A E E A L L
```
**Australian Exhibit**

```
L F I A R B E Z F S
H L W O N J L G E T
R H I N O C E R O S
O F F O T H P E P H
O N E S N O H I W I
L L J G I R A F F E
U S T S T R N A N G
L E M Y S E T L F W
```
**African Exhibit**

ZEBRA

ORANGUTAN

KOOKABURRA

ELEPHANT

KANGAROO

JAGUAR

# Famous Places

The United States has many interesting and unique places to visit. First see if you can match each of these travel sites to its state. Then find them all in the grid on the next page.

1. Grand Canyon
2. Statue of Liberty
3. Graceland
4. Mount Rushmore
5. Golden Gate Bridge
6. Everglades
7. The Capitol
8. Gateway Arch
9. Niagara Falls
10. Carlsbad Caverns
11. Hoover Dam
12. Kitty Hawk
13. Wrigley Field
14. Pearl Harbor
15. Williamsburg

6 Florida
__ Hawaii
2 New York
__ Tennessee
__ Virginia
1 Arizona
__ California
__ New Mexico
7 Washington, DC
9 New York
__ N. Carolina
__ Missouri
13 Illinois
__ S. Dakota
__ Nevada

```
I H A V G R U B S M A I L L I W E S
N S N R E V A C D A B S L R A C A T
I L W A T S W D N D T H E D T O P A
A S E E H O U N T R U C K S H M E T
G O L D E N G A T E B R I D G E A U
A R O R C I C L N V T A T E R V R E
R E A N A E G E N O T Y T O A B L O
A E L S P E V C H O W A Y T N H H F
F E Y C I A N A L H A W H S D T A L
A S E V T L V R E V E E A A C W R I
L A Y T O N A G O F R T W O A C B B
L W I T L S O N I A N A K K N S O E
S E V E R G L A D E S G T H Y A R R
W H E E R O M H S U R T N U O M N T
W R I G L E Y F I E L D T N N E Y Y
```

# Lots of Luggage

If you are vacationing far away, you might take an airplane to get there quickly. Find all the airport words listed in the luggage, then gather the leftover letters from left to right and top to bottom. They will spell out the answer to this funny knock-knock joke.

**KNOCK KNOCK**
WHO'S THERE?
**ALPACA**
ALPACA WHO?

```
D R A O B Y A
L U G G A G E
A L P W A C A
V T N H E T T
I U T F H R E
R P U G L N K
R N I K A Y C
A L Y L O U I
F P P A O C T
L E V A R T K
```

```
N O I T A N I T S E D D
S E C U R I T Y A T E H
T E R M I N A L E L S U
I T C E R U T R A P E D
S E A T A S E Y R O W !
```

ARRIVAL, BOARD, DELAY, DEPARTURE, DESTINATION,
FLIGHT, FLY, LUGGAGE, PILOT, PLANE, ROW, RUNWAY,
SEAT, SECURITY, TERMINAL, TICKET, TRAVEL

# Chapter 6

# Animal Friends

# Pets at the Vet

These animals are done at the vet. See how quickly you can get them ready to go home! What kind of traveling case is the best for each one? Hint: There are three animals in each carrier.

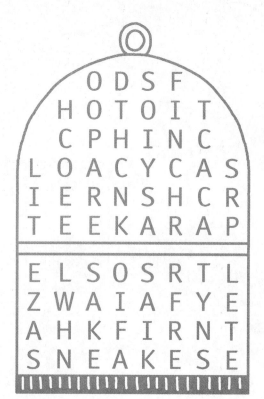

```
      O D S F
    H O T O I T
    C P H I N C
    L O A C Y C A S
    I E R N S H C R
    T E E K A R A P

    E L S O S R T L
    Z W A I A F Y E
    A H K F I R N T
    S N E A K E S E
```

GERBIL

CANARY

RABBIT

DOG

```
    P A R A K S E E T S T
    I T A R A N T U L A I
    T H I A N A K T H T S
    A B B I T K A S P I D
    H A R D S E T P A R T
    I S F D R A Z I L E L
```

# MICE

# LIZARD

# CAT

# SNAKE

# TARANTULA

# HAMSTER

# FINCH

# PARAKEET

```
    I Z M I        H A L M S T
T D O G S A      S S I M Y D O
S P I C D E      P Z A K E E I
S H E W A A G    O D R G R O D
C R A B B I T    A R S I E R P
                 D
```

```
C A N A R L Y F I C H
A B E C D I E H K I I
F I C H N B F E
H K I I G R J
H A M S T E R
R L M Q O G P
```

# Tall Tale

Giraffes are the tallest animals in the world. Find the six synonyms for the word "tall" hiding in the giraffe's neck. Then write the remaining letters from left to right and top to bottom on the dotted lines. When you are done, you will have the silly answer to the riddle!

| | | |
|---|---|---|
| G | S | O |
| N | T | T |
| O | O | H |
| L | W | E |
| Y | E | C |
| A | R | B |
| N | I | L |
| G | N | O |
| H | G | F |
| I | T | T |
| G | S | Y |
| H | M | E |
| L | L | T |
| H | Y | E |
| I | H | R |
| S | T | T |
| I | G | N |
| K | N | Y |
| F | E | E |
| E | L | T |

*"TALL" synonyms to find:*
HIGH, LOFTY, LENGTHY,
LONG, BIG, TOWERING

## Why do giraffes have long necks?

\_\_ \_\_\_ \_\_\_\_\_

\_\_\_\_' \_ _____ ,

\_\_\_\_\_ .

_____ \_\_\_\_\_ !

# Farm Fun

Each of the ten words rhymes with the name of an animal commonly found on a farm. Figure out each animal name and find it hidden in the barn.

NOW = _ _ _  COARSE = _ _ _ _ _ _

WEEP = _ _ _ _ _ _  STUCK = _ _ _ _

DIG = _ _ _  NICE = _ _ _ _ _

HAT = _ _ _  FLICK = _ _ _ _ _

JUICE = _ _ _ _ _ _

BOAT = _ _ _ _

N T
J Y C A
I W I S
H C T H R M T
A G G L I I
S N O S W O U C E O
I O S T O H D E O L
P G S K K I O N G T F G
O T A E C A U R S E B A T
H B J I S T G O O S E N E W O S
O N K E Y S N E L O Y H T L
D U C K P L E A X L S I E W
T B H U H S P O
J M I L E W O C
I S C T E O H S
F N K O P I G O
T E P Y R I T J

# Ocean Alive

Where would ocean animals be without water to live in? Using the letters W-A-T-E-R, complete the twelve animal names, then find them all beneath the waves.

CR_B            SH_IMP          S_ _ _HO_ S_

_H_L_           SH _ _ K         LOBS_ _ _

_U_ _ _L_        _ _ L            J_LLYFISH

S_ _ L          CL_M            OC_OPUS

B A R C O E L T R U T
H S E A H O R S E W C
A E T N O C T O P U S
L I S S C E O M M P H
L A B E I M L N I W A
H E O A A N I A R B R
J E L L Y F I S H A K
S I C C A L L Y S W P

# Holed Up

When the cold weather comes, many animals hole up in burrows, caves, tree trunks, or deep mud to hibernate (sleep) until the warm weather returns. These twelve animals would never hibernate together in the wild, but in this puzzle they are quite cozy together!

woodchuck

chipmunk

bat

bear

frog

turtle

squirrel

skunk

snake

ladybug

mouse

raccoon

```
      W O O D C H
    I Q U H I T W A
  Q W S I S Q U I R S
  E W O O D C H U C K N T
  L F L M U N H K A U N A U C
  I B A T M S I T U B U K R O
  D E D O O O P M A E K O T O
  Y C Y R U R M T F A S Q L L
  B A B R S Q U I R R E L E A
  G U U L E U N O O C C A R G
  S G S N A K E G I C E A
    T B E R H E M O O S
    N I T B O T W O
      U L D B E N
```

# Man's Best Friend

Choosing the right dog for your family can be quite a task. There are so many breeds to choose from! Use a highlighter to find all the dogs hidden in the grid on the following page.

| | | |
|---|---|---|
| AKITA | DALMATION | PEKINGESE |
| BASSET HOUND | DOBERMAN PINSCHER | POODLE |
| BICHON FRISE | GERMAN SHEPHERD | PUG |
| BOXER | GOLDEN RETRIEVER | ROTTWEILER |
| BULLDOG | GREAT DANE | SAINT BERNARD |
| CHIHUAHUA | GREYHOUND | SAMOYED |
| COCKER SPANIEL | IRISH SETTER | SHIH TZU |
| COLLIE | LABRADOR RETRIEVER | WHIPPET |
| DACHSUND | LHASA APSO | YORKSHIRE TERRIER |

*Which leash goes to which dog?*

**Extra Fun:** Use a dark colored marker to make a big polka dot of color over each letter X. Connect the dots to create a puppy portrait. Maybe this is the dog for you!

```
I R R E H C S N I P N A M R E B O D E
G S H I H T Z U A E N A D T A E R G L
R Y G E R M A N S H E P H E R D L L H
E O L X X P E K I N G E S E X X B A A
Y R Y M X X A T I K A X X M X A B S
H K I X S B Y X X X X X R I O X R R A
O S S X D A L M A T I O N R I X K A A
U H E D X S O X G I H X O I X P L D P
N I V X I S X O X G X O X S W X Y O S
D R X N B E X X X F X X X H H A X R O
A E X R O T T W E I L E R S I E X R D
E T X H X H S O O X U N D E P H X E R
S E X R E O I O X H X E A T P V X T A
I R X E R U N F I X T D H T E A X R N
R R B X I N G B O X N W L E T X O I R
F I F I X D C E X U X C R R X E M E E
N E E H A X X X S P A X X X M S H V B
O R I A P E D H X U X H O T T O H E T
H D L O G B C I X G X E L D O O P R N
C S L C U A I T U X O B U L L D O G I
I G O L D E N R E T R I E V E R N E A
B E C H I H U A H U A T D E Y O M A S
O C O C K E R S P A N I E L P A Y D A
```

# Cold Creatures

Break the snowflake code to find the names of ten arctic animals. Then find where they are hiding in the snow bank!

❇=A  ❋=E  ❄=I  ✳=O  ❆=U

C✳R❋B✳❆     P✳L❇R B✳✳R

H❇RP S❆AL     PT❇RM❄G❇N

L❆MM❄NG     SN✳WY ✳WL

M❋SK✳X     B❆L❆GA WH❇L❋

W✳LR❆S     ❇RCT❄C F✳X

```
T A R M                               B E
P S E E L S T I S R A I N A
R O U T P T A R M I G A N S R
A G C A R I B O U O N C E A G C
B R N N I T H I S N K S T H A T T
F E C I W I L L K N E U V E R S T I
W O L T M P O P O L A R B E A R L A C
H Y U I M E A X R M L W O Y W O N S F
A S G N E K O I S A L A E S P R A H O
L E B E L U G A W H A L E F I X I N X
```

# Desert Dwellers

Many varieties of snakes live in the desert. Some are poisonous; some are not! Find the seven species curled up together in this grid. Here's the tricky part: The names are not always spelled in a straight line! You can start at the first letter of a name and move up, down, around a corner, and side to side—but not diagonally. One has been done for you.

RATTLESNAKE          KINGSNAKE

GOPHER SNAKE         BANDED SAND SNAKE          GLOSSY SNAKE ✓

CORAL SNAKE          DESERT WORM SNAKE

D M H O R A B O N D

E R A C H L A L A X

S O T G K I N G S R

E W T L E Y D E D E

R T E O S S G O P H

# Animals in Danger

All over the world, thousands of animal species are in danger of becoming extinct. Use a marker to highlight the twenty endangered animals. Read the extra letters from left to right and top to bottom to discover some good news about one very familiar animal!

ANGEL SHARK    GAZELLE    OKAPI    ATLANTIC SALMON

BLUE WHALE    GIANT PANDA    PIKAS    GREEN SEA TURTLE

CHEETAH    GORILLA    POLAR BEAR    HIPPOPOTAMUS

CORALS    MANATEE    RHINOCEROS    MONARCH BUTTERFLY

ELEPHANT    MANTA RAY    TIGER    SNOW LEOPARD

```
D R A P O E L W O N S E F E O R U
H R I D E C A D G A Z E L L E H E
I S P A F T E R G I T T W T A I S
P R A E B R A L O P D A E R C N L
P A K R E D E P R N D N B U A O N
O N O M L A S C I T N A L T A C M
P G E R E L H D L K T M U A H E A
O E A M A E E R L R A I E E C R N
T A N R E B E A A L D S W S E O T
A A O T G G L E I S N O H N L S A
M C A G I A N T P A N D A E O N R
U H G T E R T N A H P E L E I N A
S M O N A R C H B U T T E R F L Y
D A N G E L S H A R K A N G G E R
```

Chapter 7

# Hobbies

# Cool Car Collection

Christopher loves to collect cars, wherever they are! The definitions below suggest words that all contain the letters C-A-R. Look for these words in the puzzle grid on the next page. Extra Fun: In the word search, the letters C-A-R show up as a small picture of a car instead of the letters themselves!

Short, hollow pasta = __ __ __ __ __ __ __ __

Skinny cloth worn around the neck = __ __ __ __ __

A meat eater = __ __ __ __ __ __ __ __

One-sided letter sent
   with no envelope = __ __ __ __ __ __ __ __

Orange root vegetable = __ __ __ __ __ __

An animated film = __ __ __ __ __ __ __

Bright red color = __ __ __ __ __ __ __ __

To throw away = __ __ __ __ __ __ __

Bright red bird = __ __ __ __ __ __ __ __ __

Fake person made out of straw
   = __ __ __ __ __ __ __ __ __ __

To slice meat = __ __ __ __ __

Circular, sideways handstand
   = __ __ __ __ __ __ __ __

A rug = __ __ __ __ __ __

A Christmas song = __ __ __ __ __

*ZOOM!*

X L A N I D 🚗 A 🚗 B C D 🚗
A B C D A E F G T H I J K
B L 🚗 E B M A 🚗 O N I M N
C O P O C Q R S O T U V W
D X Y F L Z A B N C D E 🚗
F I F G D G H I J K L M V
G N S H E O 🚗 N I V O R E
🚗 P Q 🚗 F R S T U V W X Y
H Z A I D B S 🚗 E C R O W
I J K L M N O P Q R S T U
P O S T 🚗 D C D 🚗 R O T V
E F 🚗 J G G H I J K L M W
N O L K H P Q S S T U V X
🚗 P E T I W 🚗 T W H E E L
X Y T L J K L M N O P Q Y
Z A B M 🚗 N O P Q S 🚗 F Z

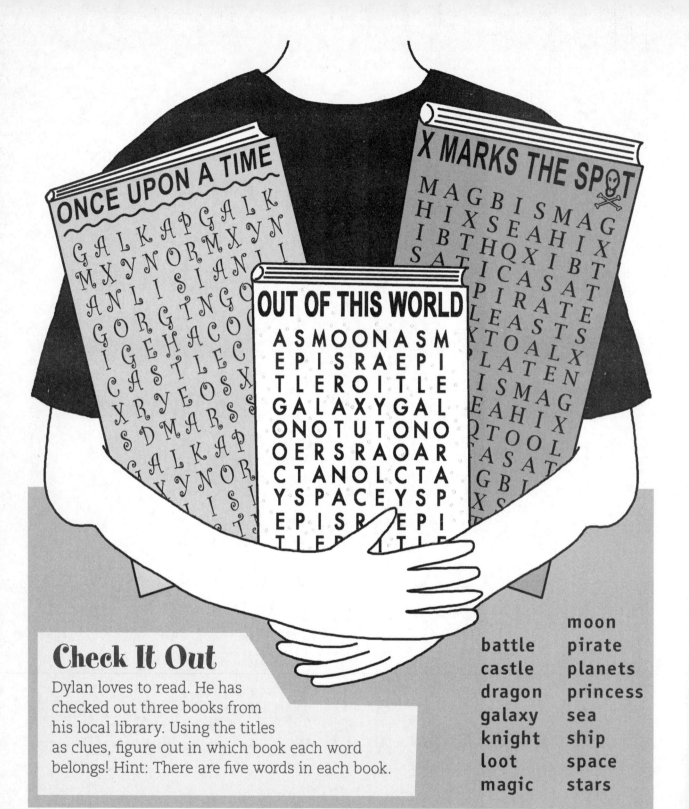

## Check It Out

Dylan loves to read. He has checked out three books from his local library. Using the titles as clues, figure out in which book each word belongs! Hint: There are five words in each book.

moon
battle    pirate
castle    planets
dragon    princess
galaxy    sea
knight    ship
loot    space
magic    stars

# Origami Animals

Take a square of paper, fold it in specific ways, and you can create all kinds of different shapes. This art form is called origami! To see some of the animals that can be made by folding a square of paper, follow these directions:

- The animal names form one long chain.
- Start by finding the word BEAR.
- The last letter of BEAR will be the first letter of the next animal.

Continue until you find all the hidden animals. Remember, the last letter of each animal is the first letter of the next animal.

**Helpful Hint:** The animals in the list are not in order!

BEAR
DOG
TURTLE
TOAD
ELEPHANT
RABBIT
GIRAFFE

R A B B I T I U S
A T A N U E B A R
E D T R O F B L E
B O T V E A T F O
D L O O R N F I A
E L E P H A N T G
M I C O R U O L F
U R T I D A I S F
T I G O D L L Y E

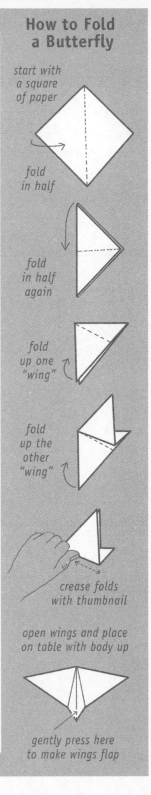

start with
a square
of paper

fold
in half

fold
in half
again

fold
up one
"wing"

fold
up the
other
"wing"

crease folds
with thumbnail

open wings and place
on table with body up

gently press here
to make wings flap

# Delicious Desserts

Brian's hobby is baking. Find the eight types of goodies that he is baking today!

**BARS, BROWNIES, CAKES, COOKIES, CUPCAKES, PIES, SQUARES, TARTS**

```
N H O N E Y P I S T A C H I H
O P U C U P C A K E S M P K I
R A S P O B E R R Y R R H U B
S E I N W O R B A S T A E V B
C H O C O L K S E K A C U L A
T T E R S C O I T C H A L Q R
C A R R O T P B E U T T E R S
E A M E O T A R T S S E W A T
U C I N N A M O N N U T M E G
```

# Aspiring Artist

Annie loves to paint and draw. Can you find her art supplies hidden in the canvas?

**Extra Fun:** Try highlighting the words in different colors!

ACRYLICS, BRUSH, CANVAS, CHARCOAL, CRAYON, DRAW, EASEL, FIGURE, INK, MARKER, OILS, PAINT, PALETTE, PAPER, PASTEL, PEN, PENCIL, SKETCH, SMOCK, STUDIO, TURPENTINE, WASH, WATERCOLOR

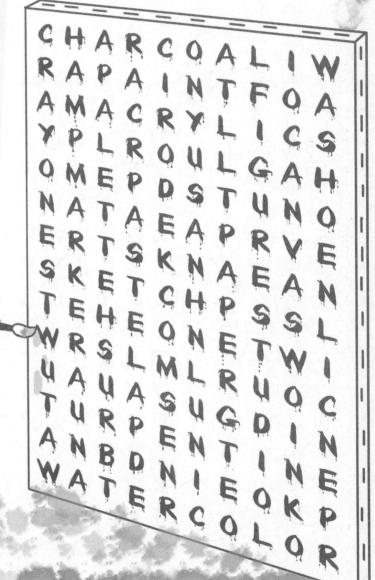

# Zap! Pow!

Lots of kids collect comic books. Not only are they great to read, it's also fun to own ones that are hard to find! Speaking of hard to find, can you spot all the superheroes hiding in the grid?

Avengers
Batman
Captain
   America
Fantastic Four
Flash
Green Lantern
Ninja Turtles
Robin
Spiderman
Superman
Transformers
Wonder Woman
X-Men

```
N I W T O I M E A R G O T O
F A N T A S T I C F O U R N
M L I O C S H B W O N D A R
E N N T A U F A M E T M N E
D I J S P P L T E N O O S T
O F A T H E A X A W R P F N
P S T A A R S M R Y I O O A
Y R U F I M T E V D O R R L
I E R T N A D N E C A O M N
T G T O B N O R N W A B E E
L N L I O T M T N I B O R E
L E E W L A U F L A S H S R
U V S L N U A N D R I C H G
C A P T A I N A M E R I C A
```

# Darling Dolls

Donna has a large collection of dolls that she has made. Her hobby is to decorate each doll to match the name it has been given! Can you find all of Donna's dolls?

```
C R Y E O B U N C
H D A I S Y H I A
E I P T R O B I N
R K E N N U R O D
R O N O N A T K Y
Y O N N T S H L I
C R Y S T A L S T
O B U N Y O S O M
C A N D H E D Y I
```

| | |
|---|---|
| HOLLY | CHERRY |
| CRYSTAL | DOT |
| BROOK | DAISY |
| ROBIN | PENNY |
| BUNNY | ROSE |
| CANDY | STAR |

**Extra Fun:** Pick your favorite name from the list and decorate this doll to match. Add hair, a hat, an apron, shoes—whatever you like!

# Stitching Time

If quilting is your hobby, you will need a lot of supplies. See if you can find all of the sewing items hidden in this quilt!

```
I W O T H I M B L E U
L D E L D E E N L O V
P O T S M A K E A Q G
P I N C U S H I O N S
A U N I L T S O I M R
T E T S I M E T J U E
T S E S F O T R M E L
E A N O D A I W O Q U
R C I R B A F U S E R
N A L S E T H R E A D
```

**THIMBLE, NEEDLE, FABRIC, THREAD, PATTERN,
SCISSORS, RULER, PINS, BATTING, PINCUSHION**

```
T H E E T I G H T E
E E T R U M P E T N T T
W E I L B V G E O R V E R E
R T M U A R N E C L O P N A I I
R E P D E L O B O E U M N I E B A I
L S A L E C G Y A T T E B K R A I D N A
N P N A M N E E R S I U A O N A I N N M G P
A I A V I O L I N S R L S N R L H A O U P L
S O C R I D H L Y S O I F R E N C H H O R N N E
L U C E O E P O A N O I G H T O S N B A D L X M
M T O D L A O B I N N P C Y M B A L S A S I P N
I N L R A G L S A E X T U B E T I O L N S R L R
A O U N D Y C E                 N Y O N E A S U
    I M T E X P                     R I D H B E
      A N D P                       R E D J
```

## In the Orchestra

Like music? There are plenty of instruments you could learn to play! Locate all of these on the stage at Symphony Hall.

**STRINGS:** *BASS, CELLO, HARP, VIOLA, VIOLIN*

**WOODWINDS:** *BASSOON, CLARINET, FLUTE, OBOE, PICCOLO, TUBA*

**BRASS:** *FRENCH HORN, TROMBONE, TRUMPET, TUBA*

**PERCUSSION:** *BASS DRUM, BELLS, CYMBALS, GONG, PIANO, SNARE DRUM, TIMPANI, TRIANGLE, XYLOPHONE*

## Saving Stamps

Collecting stamps from all over the world is a very popular hobby. Each stamp contains two letters missing from the countries listed. Fill in the blanks correctly, then find the hidden countries on the globe.

ME_ _CO

EG_ _ _T

P_ _ _U

C_ _ _NA          CA_ _ _DA

FR_ _ _CE        V_ _T_ _ _M

IN_ _ _A          AU_ _ _RA_ _ _A

SW_ _ _EN        LI_ _ _UA_ _ _A

GR_ _ _CE

Chapter 8

# Sports

# Having a Ball

All of these words are specific to basketball, tennis, or golf. Do you know which ones belong together in each ball?

```
          S T D U N
        A B O U N Z E
      S D O O W E F R O
    N E P A K B U L C N I
  L U H A N D I C A P C N V
  A T O R O E M I G B E T I
  J E L G R E E N S O K H F
  U S E Y I P U T T G F E T
  M Q S T R O K E I E I R S
    F P E I D D A C Y A N
      B I R D I E K D H
        A D T O P L A
          Y W H O E
```

*GOLF BALL*

**Extra Fun:**

Instead of circling the answers, use a magic marker to highlight each word with a single line of color!

| | | |
|---|---|---|
| ACE | DEFENSE | HANDICAP |
| ADVANTAGE | DEUCE | HOLES |
| BASKET | DRIBBLE | IRON |
| BIRDIE | DUNK | JUMP |
| BOGEY | FAULT | LOVE |
| BOUNCE | FLAGSTICK | MATCH |
| CADDIE | FOUL | NET |
| CLUB | GREEN | OFFENSE |
| COURT | GUARD | PAR |

R E B Q U
A C E C L B U
R O N B T M S T D
A D V A N T A G E L E
H C E O L E W T U K T H O
T O H L O T A C M C L G F
E U P L V T E H A A U R O
W R O E E O L V L R A E R
H T I Y L L A R R P F E T
M N I B O U N C E I T
T E I E K O R T S
N V U L L E Y
L V Y S D

*TENNIS BALL*

**POINT**

**PUTT**

**RACKET**

**RALLY**

**REBOUND**

**SERVE**

**SET**

**SHOT**

**STROKE**

**TEE**

**VOLLEY**

**WOOD**

I B P U T
W A B S T H E
O P O S I F A L L
T E T D N U O B E R O
V F A F O U L F A D G D O
O P M U J H E F S R C R P
L D E F E N S E K A O I L
L T N I O P Q N E U U B O
E O E K N U D S T G R B Y
D R I B B L E W E T L
A S T R O L E R I
R S T W O O T
P L E Y E

*BASKETBALL*

# Take Me Out to the Ballgame

Find all these baseball terms in the diamond. When you are finished, read the remaining letters from left to right and top to bottom to enjoy a funny joke!

BALK, BALL, BASE, BATTER, BENCH, BUNT, ERROR, FOUL, GLOVE, HELMET, HIT, INFIELD, INNING, MITT, MOUND, OUTFIELD, PITCHER, RUN, SLIDE, STEAL, STRIKE, TAG, TEAM, UMPIRE

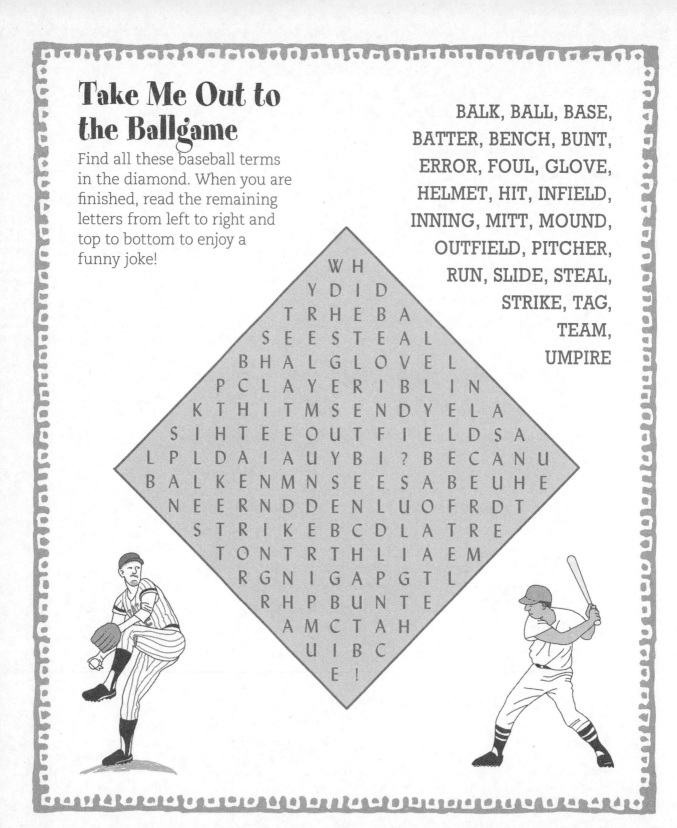

```
                W H
              Y D I D
            T R H E B A
          S E E S T E A L
        B H A L G L O V E L
      P C L A Y E R I B L I N
    K T H I T M S E N D Y E L A
  S I H T E E O U T F I E L D S A
L P L D A I A U Y B I ? B E C A N U
B A L K E N M N S E E S A B E U H E
  N E E R N D D E N L U O F R D T
    S T R I K E B C D L A T R E
      T O N T R T H L I A E M
        R G N I G A P G T L
          R H P B U N T E
            A M C T A H
              U I B C
                E !
```

G=❄  I=❄

M=❄  O=❄

R=❄

B❄ND❄N❄S

B❄❄T

C❄U❄SE

D❄❄P

F❄N❄SH

FLA❄

_____

STA❄T❄N❄

❄ATE

_____

❄❄❄UL

P❄LES

❄UN

SK❄S

SLAL❄❄

T❄❄E

## Hit the Slopes

Snowflakes have covered some of the letters in this puzzle. Break the snow code before you find the words on the downhill-ski race course!

S I F I N I S H
L E L X P E T C
A T A O M O A G
L O G S O I R I
O N G B G T T S
M E S W U I I N
T P E D L K N S
C O U R S E G T
R L I O N N G H
N E S P I O A W
U S L D O T T S
R A N N D I E L
O I T S M O F B
B E A E T I O L

# Swim Meet

Dive into this puzzle and race to see how quickly you can find all the swimming words hidden in the pool!

```
E  I  F  I  W  R  E  K  O  R  T  S  T  S  A  E  R  B  T
K  T  O  G  F  L  I  P  T  U  R  N  F  O  S  W  I  M  M
O  H  I  L  R  N  G  I  T  W  T  S  A  E  E  T  O  U  Y
R  A  O  L  E  B  E  N  R  E  K  P  S  U  R  F  A  C  E
T  T  O  N  E  D  A  E  T  C  R  P  T  M  D  A  W  L  L
S  M  E  K  S  W  L  F  O  A  A  R  M  I  O  U  H  T  D
K  Y  I  N  T  A  H  L  E  L  M  N  V  N  I  T  I  M  E
C  K  E  R  Y  T  B  N  O  H  A  E  N  D  M  Y  S  F  M
A  R  I  E  L  E  N  D  T  O  M  W  T  O  U  L  T  D  B
B  U  T  T  E  R  F  L  Y  E  P  T  H  E  N  A  L  E  R
I  S  S  H  M  E  T  S  O  G  L  O  N  E  R  T  E  O  K
```

BACKSTROKE, BLOCKS, BREASTSTROKE, BUTTERFLY, DIVE, FAST, FLIP TURN, FREESTYLE, LANE, LAP, MARK, MEDLEY, METER, POOL, RELAY, SURFACE, TIME, WATER, WHISTLE

ULOF

KUPC

CHEBN

KIRN

## Scramble

Unscramble the hockey words hidden in each puck. Find them all on the ice!

LOGA

DROBA

```
R I N A S K C U P K
H S T I C K S E S D
C K O C Q L F H T R
N A N E O E O O P A
E T E I U T U C S O
B E D E R A L F K B
X N H G O A L S O T
```

OCLKC

TICKS

SOTH

TAKES

CIE

# Spelling Ball

How many words can you find in this soccer ball grid? Start at any letter, then move from one space to the next touching space in any direction, spelling out a word as you go. You may double back and use a letter more than once in a word. For example, you may spell the word EVE.

However, you may not use the same letter twice in a row. For example, you are not allowed to spell SLEEP.

The ten-letter bonus word completes this phrase: Playing soccer is much more fun than watching _____!

SCORE:

10 words = Starter

20 words = Pro

30 words = World Cup

# Secret Soccer

Be on the lookout for the word SOCCER hiding in this grid! There is only one time where all six letters appear correctly. Look forward, backward, up, down, and diagonally.

```
S R O S O S O C C E
O O R O S O C C E S
C E C C O C C O R O
C S O C E C E S O C
R O S E R E R O S S
S S O C C O S E O O
O C C S O C E C C C
C E R O C O C C C E
C O O C S E O O S E
E C O S R O C C O S
```

# Floor Exercise

This gymnast has just finished her floor routine. Look for the circular patterns she made on the floor mat! The first letter of each word has been marked with a dot. One has been done for you.

| | MOVEMENT | HANDSTAND | DANCE |
|---|---|---|---|
| ✓ACROBATICS | SOMERSAULT | ARTISTRY | TURN |
| | CARTWHEEL | TUMBLING | JUMP |

```
J X Q P X F T· K Q J X O A· K P F
F I M· X J N X U K Q P Y X R Q P
K T F O Q X R S K J R X F X T O
N P X I V I K F X S· F T K I X J
I E X E K J Q P T X O V S V Q K
X I M I X I E L X J V M F X J I
O J· K X I E Q U C· P X E K K A Q
P F U X H I X I A X R I J X X J
Q M Q K I W K R I S X Q I R O X
X A T· S X Q T V D X T X C Q P B
K G F U P X K N X F V A· Q F X A
N Q X O M Q J A O X N V S X P T
X I P B Q A X O H· D· I K X C I X
F O L O K P O J E Q A X J Q X P
X K J A F O X O X C N O A P K J
Q X O K Q P O J O K P J Q X O P
```

# Fully Equipped

Like sports? There are plenty to choose from! Figure out each picture and letter puzzle below to come up with the names of twelve different sport activities. Then find all the names in the grid on the next page!

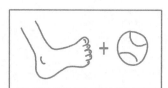

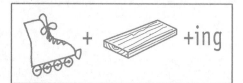

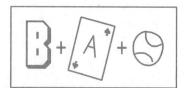

T I S I N N E T C A B N A T
E K B O E L I E V W A E R A
N A L A C R O S S E L A C J
N Y T B U C N N Y I K S H I
E A A R C H E R Y G I G I W
T K D O Y I E R D H N N E H
A I W A K T L I N T G I N L
T N U S O D A D T L H T L K
L G N I K I B A B I B A O U
F B A S K E E T A F B K A C
E O U O G I N O S T I S M R
E G O F T H I S E I K E A O
T E C T E V H K B N A C G S
B N C N B A S W A G N I I S
I B E D N A T A L E T R N J
L E R N B O L B L W E I G H
S O C K H E R L U T P O E O
A G N I D R A O B E T A K S

# Extreme Sports

X sports are action packed and very exciting! These sports often showcase the skills and spectacular tricks of individuals.

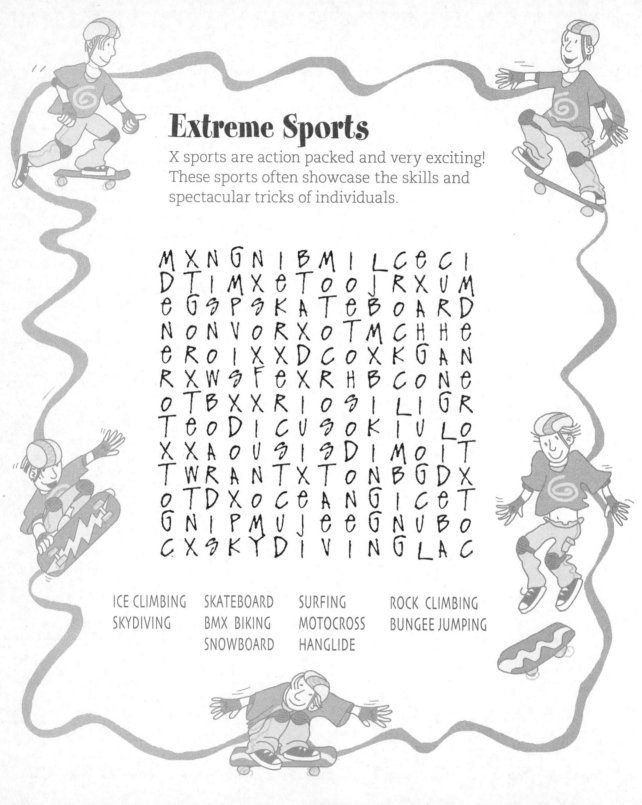

```
M X N G N I B M I L C e C I
D T I M X e T O O J R X U M
e G S P S K A T e B O A R D
N O N V O R X O T M C H H e
e R O I X X D C O X K G A N
R X W S F e X R H B C O N e
O T B X X R I O S I L I G R
T e O D I C U S O K I U L O
X X A O U S I S D I M O I T
T W R A N T X T O N B G D X
O T D X O C e A N G I C e T
G N I P M U J e e G N U B O
C X S K Y D I V I N G L A C
```

| ICE CLIMBING | SKATEBOARD | SURFING | ROCK CLIMBING |
|---|---|---|---|
| SKYDIVING | BMX BIKING | MOTOCROSS | BUNGEE JUMPING |
| | SNOWBOARD | HANGLIDE | |

Chapter 9

# Imagine That!

# Beautiful Ballerina

Emmie dreams that one day she will be a ballerina! Can you find the ten ballet words hidden in the tutu?

```
          É U
        S T Q J R W I A
      L O E U I T T É J O
      E T T E U O R I P E S Q
    É O L A J É M P T W U A E
    T S J R B A M S E Q E É C L
    E I A P O I N T E S U I O E U
    L E O T A R D E O Q E S L I T E K
    O B U A R A B E S Q U E P R T O P
    I T I O N S M U S M L R U É S O
    É O R I P U I E L A T Q P I
    N T S É Q N I B Q É I O
      P O S I T I O N S
          Q S Y
```

ARABESQUE     PLIÉ

LEOTARD     MUSIC

MIRROR     BARRE

PIROUETTE     JETÉ

POSITIONS     POINTE

# Funny Fairy

To find the silly answer to the riddle, use a dark marker to blot out the six fairy words. Collect the remaining letters from left to right and top to bottom.

F E M A L E
S T A I N D
F K G E R U
L W I N G S
Y B C E L T
S M A L L

DUST
FEMALE
FLY
MAGIC
SMALL
WINGS

What do you call a fairy who never takes a bath?

_ _ _ _ _ _ _ _ _ _ _ !

# Knight Night

Homophones are words that sound the same but are spelled differently. Words in this puzzle come in pairs—words from the list are in the knight on the right page. Find the homophones on this page!

```
S E L L F R U P
F N F Y L R M L
H A O I O O A A
R T T S W U I N
W H A L E T D E
H A I T R E E S
S T L U C R K U
E P A L O L O V
I D E W I T C H
Z R E G R O W N
E H E E R I H E
A B E A R P T D
S H I E W A A E
N I G H T W S L
O V H E D S O B
Y W T O K I G N
```

ATE
BARE
CELL
DEAR
EWE
FLOUR
GROAN
KNIGHT

KNOWS
MADE
ONE
PAUSE
PLAIN
RIGHT

ROOT
SEAS
TALE
WAIL
WAR
WHICH

*Remember: Look for these words on this page. Look for their homophones on the other page!*

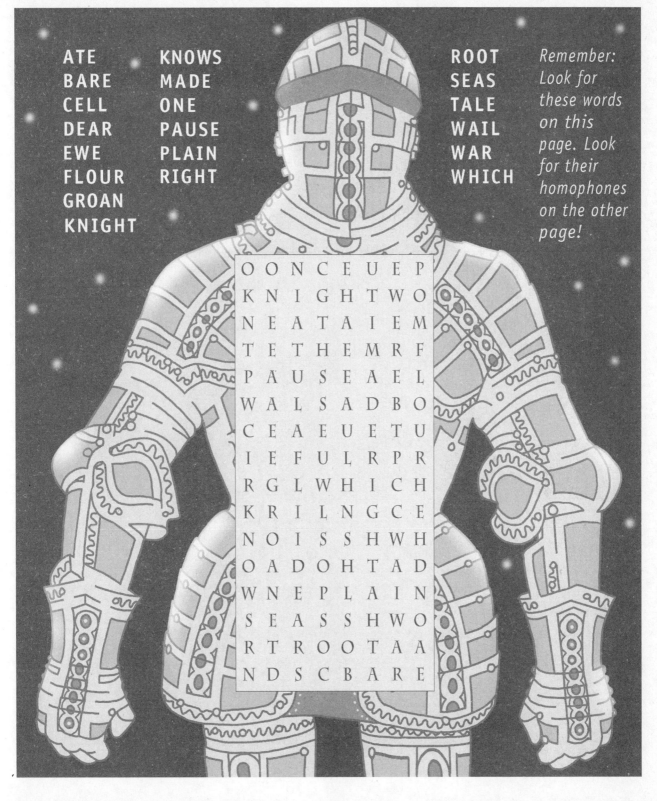

```
O O N C E U E P
K N I G H T W O
N E A T A I E M
T E T H E M R F
P A U S E A E L
W A L S A D B O
C E A E U E T U
I E F U L R P R
R G L W H I C H
K R I L N G C E
N O I S S H W H
O A D O H T A D
W N E P L A I N
S E A S S H W O
R T R O O T A A
N D S C B A R E
```

# Presto Chango

Here's your chance to be a real magician! Change the underlined letter in each word to form a new word related to magic tricks. Find these new words in the magician's hat. Hint: The pictures on this page are clues!

change W<u>I</u>ND to W__ND

change <u>F</u>UNNY to __UNNY

change <u>S</u>LOWER to __LOWER

change ST<u>I</u>R to ST__R

change <u>C</u>AT to __AT

change R<u>I</u>PE to R__PE

change SCAR<u>E</u> to SCAR__

change CAR<u>T</u>S to CAR__S

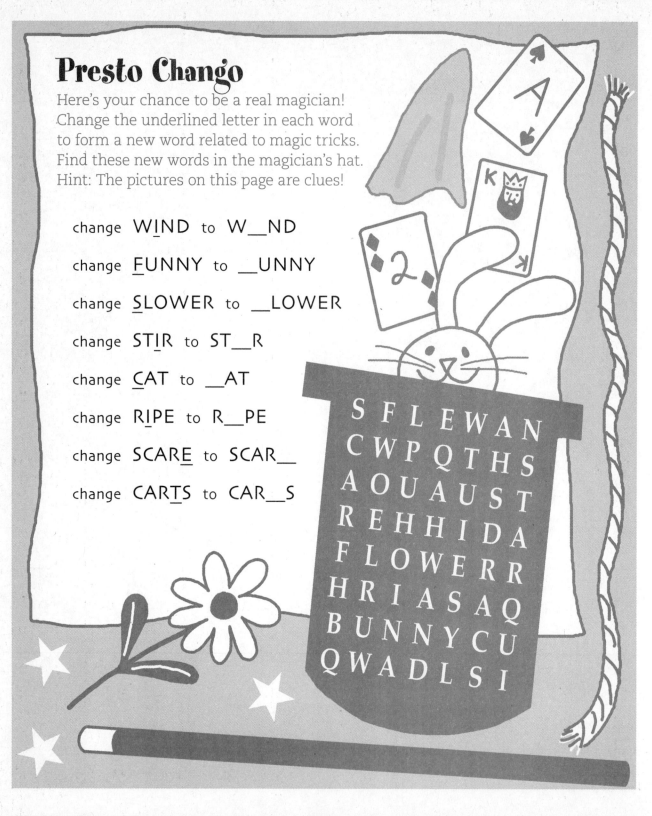

S F L E W A N
C W P Q T H S
A O U A U S T
R E H H I D A
F L O W E R R
H R I A S A Q
B U N N Y C U
Q W A D L S I

# Unusual Unicorn

This unicorn is amazed at all the words that have the letters U-N-I. Figure out each word by using the definitions, then find them all in the grid.

Special clothes that identifies a team = <u>U</u> <u>N</u> <u>I</u> _ _ _ _

All of outer space and everything in it = <u>U</u> <u>N</u> <u>I</u> _ _ _ _

All the people in your city or town = _ _ _ _ <u>U</u> <u>N</u> <u>I</u> _ _

Imaginary animal with one horn = <u>U</u> <u>N</u> <u>I</u> _ _ _ _

Gathering of old classmates = _ _ <u>U</u> <u>N</u> <u>I</u> _ _

Long shirt that hangs to the knees = _ <u>U</u> <u>N</u> <u>I</u> _

One-wheeled bike = <u>U</u> <u>N</u> <u>I</u> _ _ _ _ _

Common summer plant with trumpet-shaped
    flowers = _ _ _ <u>U</u> <u>N</u> <u>I</u> _

To join together = <u>U</u> <u>N</u> <u>I</u> _ _

Only one of its kind = <u>U</u> <u>N</u> <u>I</u> _ _ _

```
U I U D E O C O M M U N I T Y T H
I N N T K U T H A N K I T D U O R
U D I S T P U N I Q U E I W Q I E
P N F V L I G C E E L C Y C I N U
U T O T E H O W O R D I I M N U N
N I R Z E R I P E T U N I A U T I
S W M A N Y S T O O U H A R Z O O
Q U I Z P I D E Y T D O Q U I L N
```

# Pirate Booty

Can you find this pirate's buried treasure? You'll have to dig around fer the seven precious gems and metals because he'll not be giving you a list—AAARRRR!

1. _____
2. _____
3. _____
4. _____
5. _____
6. _____
7. _____

```
B O N E S G M A
R G P I C O L A
E M E R A L D S
V B A O F D M A
L O R P M O S P
I T L R U E M P
S T S T I S E H
Y L K B S C H I
D E U A D M A R
N R S K U L L E
D I A M O N D S
X W A R N I N G
```

# Marvelous Mermaids

Want to learn a bit about mermaids? Fit each word into its proper place in the paragraph. Then find each word in the giant clamshell!

**ENCHANT, LEGEND, LOVELY, OCEAN, SING, SWIM, TAIL, UNDERWATER**

Mermaids are

_____

fish-women that

live _____

in the _____.

They have a _____

instead of legs,

and can _____

really fast.

_____ says

that mermaids

can _____

sailors when they

_____.

```
J K C O M A E K I
C I N G B U I R D O L
A O C E A N S Y D N U
M S A N O D V L G O S
E A H C L E G E N D T
R L D H S R E V I T H
M A I A Y W L O S E A
J V O N T A I L I C Y
C A T C T L M E A
  Q U E S R
  I M R E R
    E O Y
```

# Ask an Alien

Imagine talking with a creature from another planet! Fit the letters A-L-I-E-N into the missing spaces to create some outer space sentences!

**Extra Fun:** How many UFOs can you find in this puzzle?

"Take me to your L_ _ _D_ _R!"

"Which one of the P_ _ _N_ _TS do you live on?"

"What fuel do you use in your SP_ _C_ _SH_ _P?"

"There are billions of S T_ R S in just one galaxy!"

"What kind of T_ _CH_ _O_ _OGY did you use to build your spaceship?"

"The U_ _ _ _V_ _RS_ _ is full of stars and galaxies!"

"What are those strange, flashing _ _ IGHTS?"

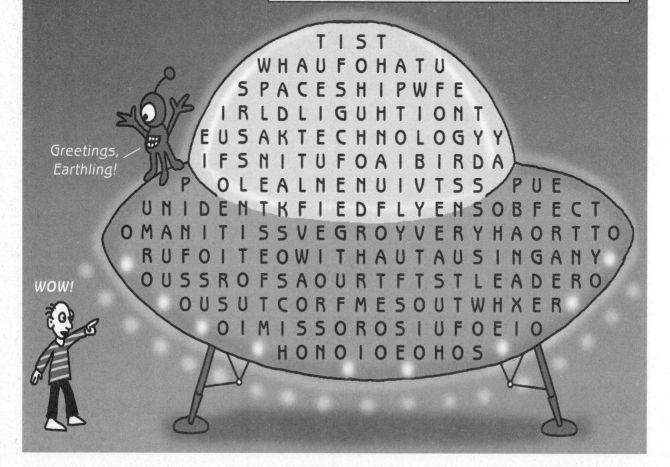

Greetings, Earthling!

WOW!

```
        T I S T
      W H A U F O H A T U
    S P A C E S H I P W F E
    I R L D L I G U H T I O N T
    E U S A K T E C H N O L O G Y Y
    I F S N I T U F O A I B I R D A
  P   O L E A L N E N U I V T S S   P U E
  U N I D E N T K F I E D F L Y E N S O B F E C T
  O M A N I T I S S V E G R O Y V E R Y H A O R T T O
  R U F O I T E O W I T H A U T A U S I N G A N Y
  O U S S R O F S A O U R T F T S T L E A D E R O
  O U S U T C O R F M E S O U T W H X E R
    O I M I S S O R O S I U F O E I O
      H O N O I O E O H O S
```

# Custom Castles

A castle is an enormous building with many parts. See if you can find all the castle words hidden in the castle wall!

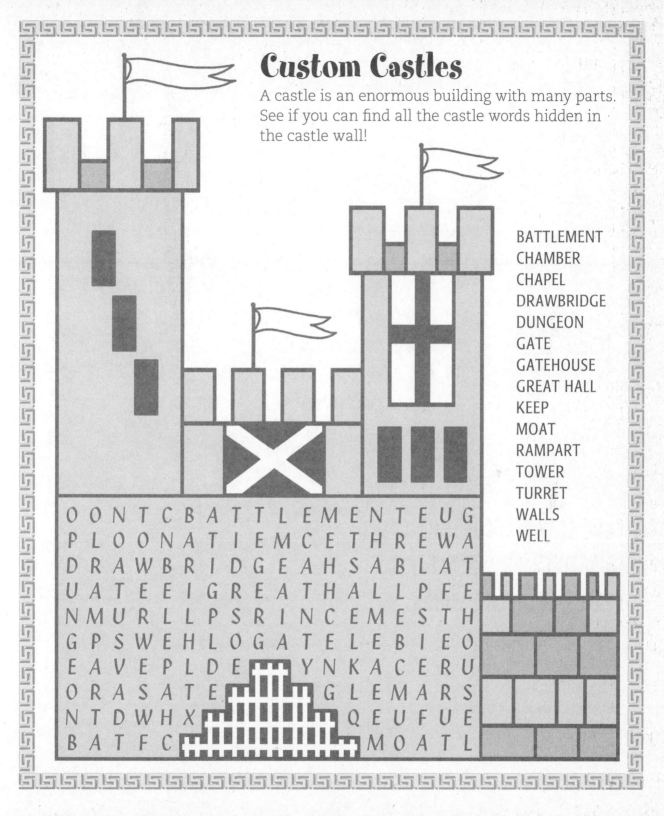

BATTLEMENT
CHAMBER
CHAPEL
DRAWBRIDGE
DUNGEON
GATE
GATEHOUSE
GREAT HALL
KEEP
MOAT
RAMPART
TOWER
TURRET
WALLS
WELL

O O N T C B A T T L E M E N T E U G
P L O O N A T I E M C E T H R E W A
D R A W B R I D G E A H S A B L A T
U A T E E I G R E A T H A L L P F E
N M U R L L P S R I N C E M E S T H
G P S W E H L O G A T E L E B I E O
E A V E P L D E Y N K A C E R U
O R A S A T E G L E M A R S
N T D W H X Q E U F U E
B A T F C M O A T L

```
S O N S C E U P T O W N A T I
S O M C E T F I R E H I E T R
E S A A L L W A E S A F N R I
C E R L C A E D A R A A O G O
N G N E W I W H S U I L P R S
I N I S I R N S U G O G L Y
R T W A E S A V R C E I T A R
P I A V N H E R E P T I L E
O L A A T E H I J
N C Y M Y T H S
A Y A N D D A G
```

**CAVE, CLAWS, COLOR, FIRE, GIANT, LAIR, MYTH, PRINCESS, REPTILE, SCALES, TREASURE, WINGS**

## Dragon Breath

This brave knight is about to do battle with a fierce dragon. Can you find the hidden words before the dragon's flames burn the knight?

# The Wrap-Up Puzzle

# Look Again!

Thought you were done hunting for things? Not so fast! See if you can spot each of these picture pieces somewhere in this book. Write the name of the puzzle each piece is from in the space under each box. Hint: There is only one piece from each chapter!

1.

2.

3.

4.

5.

6.

7. *crease folds with thumbnail*

8.

9.

# Resources

If you can't get enough of word searches, there are many Web sites available for instantaneous fun. Some of the sites require you to print out the puzzles, but others are interactive and let you solve them with your mouse. We've listed some of our favorite Web sites for you to explore:

## Discovery Education's Puzzlemaker

Create your own word search puzzles to print out and solve at home. Using the easy, step-by-step directions, you choose a title, hidden message (optional), size (number of squares in the grid), and the words. The Web site does the rest, including a solution page. In addition to creating word searches, you can also create a number of other puzzles such as cryptograms, crisscrosses, and mazes. Technical help is available.

→ *http://puzzlemaker.school.discovery.com*

## Education Place: Kids' Place Web Word Find

Publisher Houghton Mifflin hosts this interactive site complete with sound effects. Click your mouse on the first letter of a word and drag the circle over the whole word. If you are correct, you hear a "ding" and the word disappears from the list. If you are wrong, you hear a "buzz" and have to try again. Topics are seasonal. Other types of puzzles for kids are also available on this site. Brain Teasers (problem solving) and Fake Out (word definitions) are two examples.

→ *www.eduplace.com/kids/wwf*

## Mensa for Kids: Word Roundup

This word search puzzle is changed five times a week. It has an online timer so you can see how quickly you can find all the words. Rather than giving you a word list, you are provided with a set of clues of types of words to find. For example, in one puzzle you might need to search for two Greek gods, five state capitals, four vegetables, and six animals with four legs. Each time you find a correct word, a box gets checked and you receive a star next to that category when you have found all of the words in it. There is a great hint feature to help you out, and you have the option of resetting the game when you are done to try and complete it in a faster time. Mensa has other games for kids on the same site.

→ www.mensaforkids.org

## Merriam-Webster's Word Central

Although this award-winning site may not have word searches, if you are a kid who loves words, you will definitely want to visit it. Designed like a school, it has different class-rooms to explore and word-related activities to try. You can look up words in the online student dictionary, view the daily buzzword, make up your own new words, encode and decode messages, and even create silly poetry. The site is visually appealing and very easy to navigate.

→ http://wordcentral.com

## Puzzle-Club.com

This site includes printable word searches for children on many different topics and in a range of difficulty levels. The puzzles are divided into Super-Easy, Easy, Medium, and Hard. Topics included are nature, holidays, school, and other kid-friendly themes.

→ www.puzzle-club.com/kids-word-search-puzzles.html

# Puzzle Answers

E GG S & B AC O N

M I L K & C OO K I E S

B RE A D & B U TT E R

A P PLE S & O R A N G E S

P E A N U T B U TT E R & J E L L Y

S P AG H E TT I & M E A T B A L L S

CH EE S E & C R A C K E R S

S T R A W B E RR I E S & C R E A M

L E TT U C E & T O M A T O

H A M & C H EE S E

F RE N C H F R I E S & K E T C H U P

H O T D O G S & H A M B U R G E R S

Dynamic Duos • Pages 2–3

```
X M M I L K K H A M J S
S S T K T X O Q K W X T
P E A N U T B U T T E R
A W J Q D X J R G S J A
G J Q O G W T K E G J W
H E G G S T J E T A G B
E S J T G Q H K Q P D E
T X W B A C A N G P G R
T J K Q G K W X G L X R
I W X L E T T U C E G I
R K J W J Q T Q T S J E
S F R E N C H F R I E S
```

```
X C O O K I E S J J G C
S K R Y J K G H E Y K R
R M E A T B A L L S U E
E G J H C Q E J L Q K A
G H J G H K S K Y H J M
R J H Y H E E H U K S M
U Q B U T T E R J G E G
B Q G Y H C H H S I G H
M A Q K G H C H Q K N Y
A K C K J U H Y K G A H
H Y H O H P H J Y H R Y
G H Q G N K O T A M O T
```

## Lotsa Laundry • Page 4

```
B W E O S C W
S H S B L A U N O
O B O C W P S P U G B
I S E C H G A O A N P E P
W S G S O B N C J D G O E
G B O B P S T K A E B O S
I C W E C E S S M R W S C
P H B S O H A T A W E B P
B C I D B L O U S E S P S
O S R T O W E L S A G S C
E Y S H E E T S R T E
I G W C Q O G W B
B H S C B O E
```

## A sock!

## Trail of Toys • Page 6

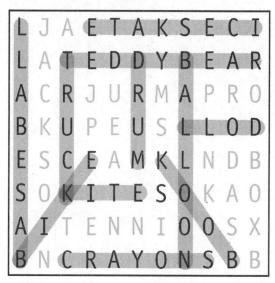

```
L J A E T A K S E C I
L A T E D D Y B E A R
A C R J U R M A P R O
B K U P E U S L L O D
E S C E A M K L N D B
S O K I T E S O K A O
A I T E N N I O O S X
B N C R A Y O N S B B
```

## Cutting the Cake • Page 5

```
C L A S S M A T E O F U T F
E F T S R O B H G I E N O T
G R A N D M A M J F S C F U
R I E S O F U E O J S L A F
A E U H J E O F K T U E T S
N N E O T J B I R T H J H E
D D T F U O L A M Y D E E T
P S I S T E R I G Y A J R O
A U N T F S S B E O F E U F
    N I S U O C U E
```

The birthday girl's name is: Amy

# Puzzle Answers

## Bathroom Humor • Page 7

L W T H O S R O R R I M
A H O T O I L E T T O E
U S Y A P N L W A H H D
N U S Y M K S S T E A I
D R E A A L S T H R I C
R B U T H T A B P R N I
Y H S E S S O A O B N E
B T H S P I O T N R U C
A O O T O S H H E E U A
S O W B C L A M T T S A
K T E H U E F A R E H B
E B R O P W A T E R O I
T M M ? R O O B B E R N
  D U T O O T H P A S T E
  C K Y ! C S E U S S I T

The extra letters read: Who always steals the soap in the bathroom? Robber Ducky!

## Perfect Pets • Page 8

BIRD
CAT
HORSE
SNAKE
MOUSE
DOG
FISH
BUNNY
*TURTLE

## Going Batty • Page 9

There are more than 30 bats in the attic. Good luck counting them all!

## More Chores! • Page 10

D R U B B E R G L O V E S
U O N V C E U P O N A D C
S T T R A S H B A G E I R
T M E T H C R E R E E W U
P E E W S O U A W S A P B
A O R I O P N U O C E R S
N N L M A M L E M D U A E
T P A I L B E E T S H G G
O O H N S P E R H B Y E N
B M Y S A H T F R I D E O
N G D O J E N N Y I L P
I V S E D N E D U S T X S

113

## Fun for Frank • Page 11

## Five-Day Forecast • Pages 14–15

### Monday

```
C H I B L Y H
F A I R I C O
S T E E R O S
W S S E A O U
T W Y Z N L Y
E R E Y I I N
D R W R M D N
```

### Tuesday

```
I C L O U D Y
S H O W E R S
W I R A N I I
A L W T E Z W
R L E O L Z N
N Y L V E L D
R N Y A I E Y
```

### Wednesday

```
A C P H Z Y L
U O O W A R N
D Y U N W E T
M I R A I N Y
L G I H N T W
D I N T D H S
T A G R Y S A
```

### Thursday

```
A B R O W R H
U R N D A O T
M I L D M I Y
T G W H R N O
W H Y A N R H
E T E U M Y T
W S S W A R M
```

### Friday

```
B O R W R M I
R H A Z Y S C
G U O I K P L
T M T T C O D
M I R A I U Y
O D M E T N I
H T O C S G A
```

## Movie Night • Page 12

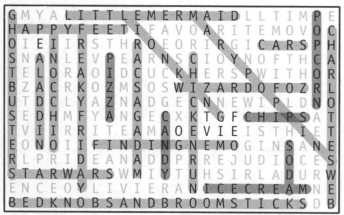

```
G M Y A L I T T L E M E R M A I D L L T I M P E
H A P P Y F E E T I F A V O A R I T E M O V O C H
O I E I I R S T H R O E O R I R G I C A R S P C H A
S N A N L E V P E A R N S C I O Y N O F T H C A R
T E L O R A O I D C U C K H E R S P W I T H O R L O
B Z A C R K O Z M S O S W I Z A R D O F O Z N D O
U T D C L Y A Z N A D G E C N N E W I P L D N
S E D H M F Y A N G E C X K T G F C H I P S A T
T V I I R R I T E A M A O E V I E I S T H I E T
E O N O I I F I N D I N G N E M O G I N S A N E
R L P R I D E A N A D D P R R E J U D I O C E S
S T A R W A R S W M I Y T U H S I R L A D U R W
E N C E O V L I V I E R A N I C E C R E A M N E
B E D K N O B S A N D B R O O M S T I C K S D B
```

Kids love to munch on: PIZZA, CANDY,
SODA, ICE CREAM, CHIPS and POPCORN.

# Puzzle Answers

## Backyard Birds • Page 16

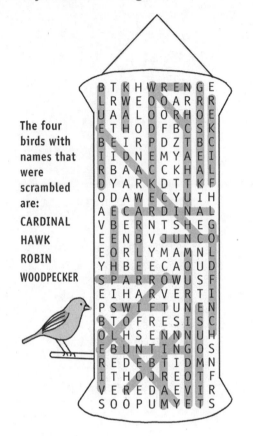

The four birds with names that were scrambled are:

CARDINAL

HAWK

ROBIN

WOODPECKER

```
B T K H W R E N G E
L R W E O O A R R R
U A A L O O R H O E
E T H O D F B C S K
B E I R P D Z T B C
I I D N E M Y A E I
R B A A C C K H A L
D Y A R K D T T K F
O D A W E C Y U I H
A E C A R D I N A L
V B E R N T S H E G
E E N B V J U N C O
E O R L Y M A M N L
Y H B E E C A O U D
S P A R R O W U S F
E I H A R V E R T I
P S W I F T U N E N
B T O F R E S I S C
O L H S E N N N U H
E B U N T I N G O S
R E D E B T I D M N
I T H O J R E O T F
V E R E D A E V I R
S O O P U M Y E T S
```

## Going Buggy • Page 17

```
W K C I T H Y D O
B E O E E E B G S
B U C Z F Z U R ?
O B K E L B T E C
T A R U Y E T D E
I S O D E E E I T
U T A H E T R P I
Q L C Y C L F S M
S T H A A E L F R
O G N A T N Y T E
M W H A I S T L T
D R A G O N F L Y
E Y L F E R I F !
```

Extra letters spell: Why do bees buzz? Because they can't whistle!

## Obstacle Course Opposites • Page 18

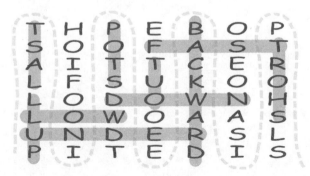

## Great Gardens • Page 19

```
M A R I G O L D
W E E D E W E E
R D W P R E T E
O Y S I A D E Y
S D W L N E L S
E E D U I W O N
E P E T U N I A
M U M E M D V P
```

```
T N A L P G G E W
Z E L E T T U C E
U E D W O E E D C
C U C U M B E R A
C W E E A D N W R
H E E D T R W E R
I E D P O T A T O
N W E C E D W E T
I E R E P P E P D
```

# The EVERYTHING KIDS' Word Search Puzzle and Activity Book

**Fantastic Fort • Page 20**

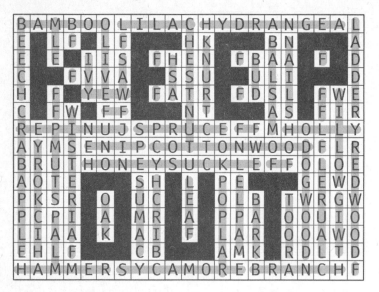

**Outdoor Eating • Page 22**

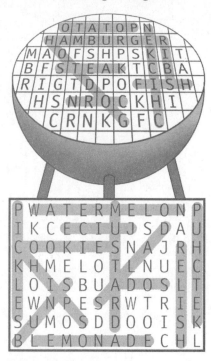

**Ready to Ride • Page 21**

**Hide & Seek • Page 23**

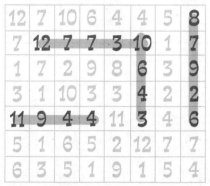

| | | | | | | | |
|---|---|---|---|---|---|---|---|
| 12-7-7-3-10 | **WOODS** | | | | | | |
| 11-9-4-4 | **TREE** | | | | | | |
| 10-6-4-3 | **SHED** | | | | | | |
| 8-7-9-2-6 | **PORCH** | | | | | | |

| 12 | 7 | 10 | 6 | 4 | 4 | 5 | 8 |
|---|---|---|---|---|---|---|---|
| 7 | 12 | 7 | 7 | 3 | 10 | 1 | 7 |
| 1 | 7 | 2 | 9 | 8 | 6 | 3 | 9 |
| 3 | 1 | 10 | 3 | 3 | 4 | 2 | 2 |
| 11 | 9 | 4 | 4 | 11 | 3 | 6 |
| 5 | 1 | 6 | 5 | 2 | 12 | 7 | 7 |
| 6 | 3 | 5 | 1 | 9 | 1 | 5 | 4 |

# Puzzle Answers

## Driveway Fun • Page 24

## Hop on the Bus • Page 26

## School Stuff • Page 27

## Plenty of Pals • Page 28

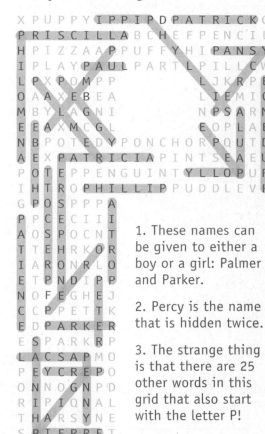

1. These names can be given to either a boy or a girl: Palmer and Parker.

2. Percy is the name that is hidden twice.

3. The strange thing is that there are 25 other words in this grid that also start with the letter P!

**What's in the Backpack? • Page 29**

**You're It! • Page 31**

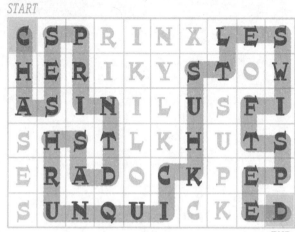

**Shape Up! • Page 30**

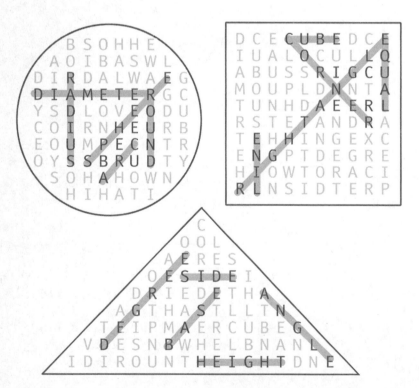

**Got Art? • Page 32**

# Puzzle Answers

## Janitor's Closet • Page 33

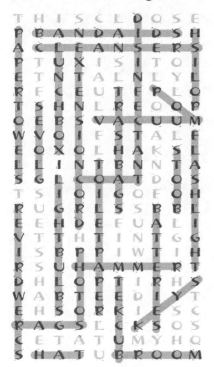

## Lunch Line • Pages 34–35

## Detention! • Page 36

The extra letters spell:
Why was the magnet
given detention? He had
a negative attitude!

## Around Town • Pages 38–39

1. LIBRARY
2. POLICE
3. VET
4. GROCERY STORE
5. CHURCH
6. POST OFFICE
7. DOCTOR
8. HARDWARE STORE
9. BANK
10. HAIRDRESSER
11. MOVIE THEATER
12. FIREFIGHTERS

# The EVERYTHING KIDS Word Search Puzzle and Activity Book

## Savings Sum • Page 40

There are 4 pennies, 3 nickels, 6 dimes, and 7 quarters for a total of $2.54.

## Love Letter • Page 41

*Roses are red,*
*Violets are blue,*
*Sugar is sweet,*
*and so are you!*

## In the Bag • Page 42

### The one food item not in the bags? Cookies. Darn!

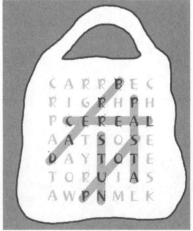

# Puzzle Answers

## Snip! Snip! • Page 43

*Words to search for:*

HEARS
EARS
HAIR
AIR
INK
IN
COB
RIM
LIP
PIN

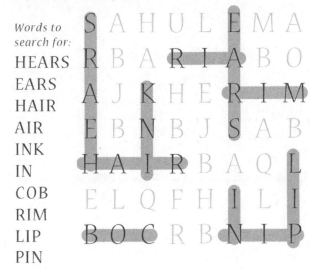

## On Fire! • Pages 44–45

FIREPLACE
FIREFLY
WILDFIRE
FIRECRACKER
FIREHOUSE
FIREPROOF
FIREWOOD
CAMPFIRE
FIRE ENGINE
BACKFIRE
FIRE EXTINGUISHER
FIREWORKS
FIREFIGHTER

## Handy Hardware • Page 46

## Road Trip • Page 48

```
        H S H O
    O S N A C K S
    U S U I T C A S E
    J I U S E I C R E S B
  O C T I K Y D O E T S O X G
  O A I C D E O O M K O O B L L
  J K S A S U N G L A S S E S A O
  S E J O O U O W R C O O L E R W D
  E S Y A D N M A P T H A N K Y O U
  T U   I L O H K N A B   B E
```

Words to look for: BOOK, CAMERA, COOLER, DOG, JACKET, MAP, MONEY, MUSIC, SNACKS, SUITCASE, SUNGLASSES

## New Hampshire Holiday • Page 49

```
X L R T R O P R I A R P A R K H
E L E V A T I O N E E T O W N I
T X V P A R K   F R R D E P H T G
I M I L E S S K I A R E A O S H
S E R T E G O L F C O U R S E W
P O R I S P R A P I B D K P R A
M I T D P A R K   E N T H E I O Y
A I A P A R K E G C L L O T F G
C O V E R E D B R I D G E A R A
R N I A T N U O M P A R K L N I
```

## Motor Messages • Page 50

```
N L O Z I S L A R O F E M I T E H T R
Y O U A R E W O N D E R F U L T H Z W
G V O O D M E N T O C O M E T O A I H
O E D I W A N T T O B U G Y O U O G O
H T F T H E I R P A R T Y I B E L R L
D O I E B E S E E I N G Y O U V E E E
E L T H I S S I T H E T S E B R A A N
W A I T F O R M E N D O M U O H T T U
A U G H T O T A R E N E G R I N T T B
R G H E W O T O O D U M B T O K N O W
I H R L D L Z Z U P S I H T E K I S C
F M I W O N D E R W O H J E N Z L E H
Z I P P I T Y D O O D A H Y W I L E O
O L L I N N A E N E R I T C O L U Y L
R G O T T O F I C R A Z Y F O R Y O U
E H T O N A T O O R R F I T A R D U T
```

## Under the Big Top • Page 51

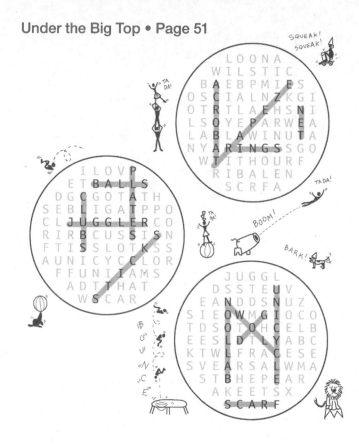

```
            L O O N A
            W I L S T I C
        B A E B P M I E S
        O S C I A L N Z K G I
        O T R T L A E H S N I
        L S O Y E P A R W E A
        L A B L A W I N U T A
        N Y A R I N G S S G O
        W T I T H O U R F
        R I B A L E N
        S C R F A
```

```
        I L O V P
        E T B A L L S
    D G C G O T A T H
    S E B L I G A T P P O
    C L J U G G L E R C O
    R I R B C U S S I S N
    F T I S S L O T K S S
    A U N I C Y C C L O R
    F F U N I I A M S
    A D T T H A T
    W S C A R
```

```
        J U G G L
        D S S T E U V
    E A N D D S N U Z
    S I E O W M G I O C O
    T D S O T O H C E L B
    E E S L D T L Y A B C
    K T W L F R A C E S E
    S V E A R S A L W M A
    S T B H E P E A R
    A K E E T S X
        S C A R F
```

## Gearing Up • Page 52

```
I L B A C K S S T O O B G N I K I H
K A E O O U A E B I N O S E D T O L
B N E T V E I H T H I K N G O C O C
O T P M E P D C I N B A C K P A C K
O E I B E N K T G F O O R B A N L I
S R F I R S T A I D K I T I E T A P
T N N E T I C M K S C A B N M E N P
S R A L U C O N I B C C O O L E R I
B O C K P O C K R A W L O D A N L C
O S L E E P I N G B A G T B O O H K
```

# Puzzle Answers

## Sunny Seashore • Page 53

## Sail Away • Page 54

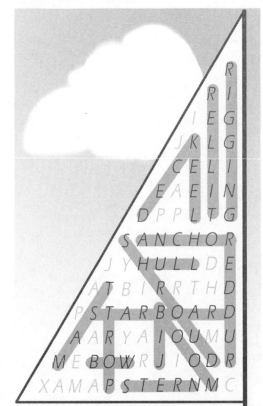

## What a Zoo! • Page 55

South American Exhibit

Australian Exhibit

African Exhibit

## Famous Places • Pages 56–57

6 Florida
14 Hawaii
2 New York
3 Tennessee
15 Virginia
1 Arizona
5 California
10 New Mexico
7 Washington, DC
9 New York
12 N. Carolina
8 Missouri
13 Illinois
4 S. Dakota
11 Nevada

**Lots of Luggage • Page 58**

KNOCK KNOCK
WHO'S THERE?
**ALPACA**
ALPACA WHO?

ALPACA THE TRUNK,
YOU PACK-A THE SUITCASE!

**Pets at the Vet • Pages 60–61**

**Tall Tale • Page 62**

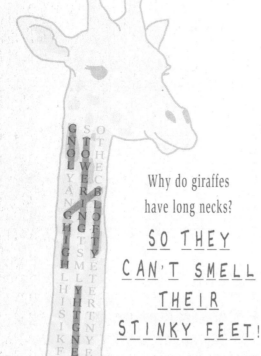

Why do giraffes
have long necks?

SO THEY
CAN'T SMELL
THEIR
STINKY FEET!

**Farm Fun • Page 63**

COW, SHEEP, PIG, BAT, HORSE,
DUCK, MICE, CHICK, GOOSE, GOAT

# Puzzle Answers

## Ocean Alive • Page 64

CRAB, WHALE, TURTLE, SEAL, SHRIMP, SHARK, EEL, CLAM, SEAHORSE, LOBSTER, JELLYFISH, OCTOPUS

```
B A R C O E L T R U T
H S E A H O R S E W C
A E T N O C T O P U S
L I S S C E O M M P H
L A B E I M L N I W A
H E O A A N I A R B R
J E L L Y F I S H A K
S I C C A L L Y S W P
```

## Man's Best Friend • Pages 66–67

```
I R R E H C S N I P N A M R E B O D E
G S H I H T Z U A E N A D T A E R G L
R Y G E R M A N S H E P H E R D L L H
E O L X P E K I N G E S E X B A A
R Y X A T I K A X X M X R A
H K I X S B Y X X R I O X R R A
O S X D A L M A T I O N R I X A A
U H E D X S O G I H X O I X P L D P
N I V X I S X O X G O X S W X Y O S
D R X N B E X F X X X H H A X R O
A E X R O T T W E I L E R S I E X R D
E T X H X H S Q O X U N D E P H X A N
S E X R E O I O X H X E A T P V X T A
I R X E R U N F I X T D H T E A X R N
R B X I N G B O X N W L E T X O I R
F I X D C E X U X C R R X E M E E
N E E H A X X X S P A X X M S H V B
E R I A P E D H X U X H O T T O H E T
H D L O G B C I X G X E L D O O P R N
C S L C U A I T U X O B U L L D O G I
I G O L D E N R E T R I E V E R N E A
B E C H I H U A H U A T D E Y O M A S
O C O C K E R S P A N I E L P A Y D A
```

## Holed Up • Page 65

```
      W O O D C H
   I Q U H I T W A
  Q W S I S Q U I R S
 E W O O D C H U C K N T
 L F L M U N H K A U N A U C
 I B A T M S I T U B U K R O
 D E D O O P M A E K O T O
 Y C Y R U R M T F A S Q L L
 B A B R S Q U I R R E L E A
 G U U L E U N O O C C A R G
 S G S N A K E G I C E A
   T B E R H E M O O S
     N I T B O T W O
       U L D B E N
```

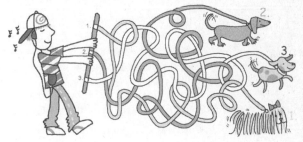

# The EVERYTHING KIDS' Word Search Puzzle and Activity Book

## Cold Creatures • Page 68

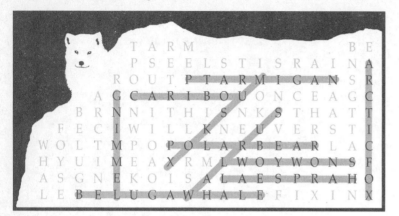

## Desert Dwellers • Page 69

## Animals in Danger • Page 70

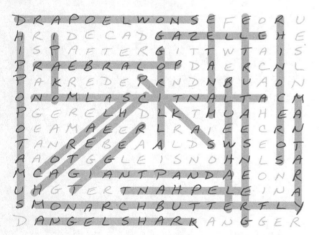

The extra letters spell: "Four decades after it was declared endangered, the American bald eagle is no longer in danger!"

## Cool Car Collection • Pages 72–73

MACARONI
SCARF
CARNIVORE
POSTCARD
CARROT
CARTOON
SCARLET
DISCARD
CARDINAL
SCARECROW
CARVE
CARTWHEEL
CARPET
CAROL

# Puzzle Answers

**Check It Out • Page 74**

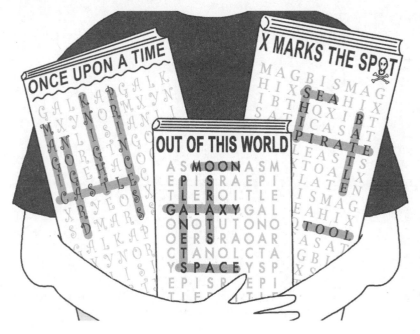

**Origami Animals • Page 75**

**Delicious Desserts • Page 76**

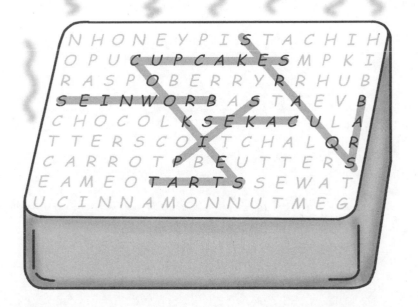

**Aspiring Artist • Page 77**

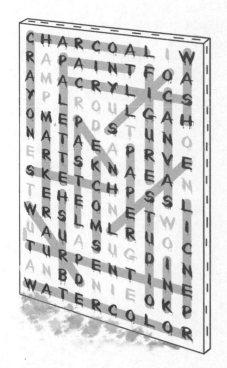

# The EVERYTHING KIDS' Word Search Puzzle and Activity Book

## Zap! Pow! • Page 78

```
N I W T O I M E A R G O T O
F A N T A S T I C F O U R N
M L I O C S H B W O N D A R
E N N T A U F A M E T M N E
D I J S P P L T E N O O S T
O F A T H E A X A W R P F N
P S T A A R S M R Y I O O A
Y R U F I M T E V D O R R L
I E R T N A D N E C A O M N
T G T O B N O R N W A B E E
L N L I O T M T N I B O R E
L E E W L A U F L A S H S R
U V S L N U A N D R I C H G
C A P T A I N A M E R I C A
```

## Darling Dolls • Page 79

```
C R Y E O B U N C
H D A I S Y H I A
E I P T R O B I N
R K E N N U R O D
R O N O N A T K Y
Y O N N T S H L I
C R Y S T A L S T
O B U N Y O S O M
C A N D H E D Y I
```

## Stitching Time • Page 80

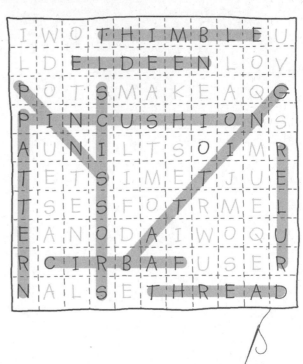

```
I W O T H I M B L E U
L D E L D E E N L O V
P O T S M A K E A Q G
P I N C U S H I O N S
A U N I L T S O I M R
T E T S I M E T J U E
T S E S F O T R M E L
E A N O D A I W O Q U
R C I R B A F U S E R
N A L S E T H R E A D
```

## In the Orchestra • Page 81

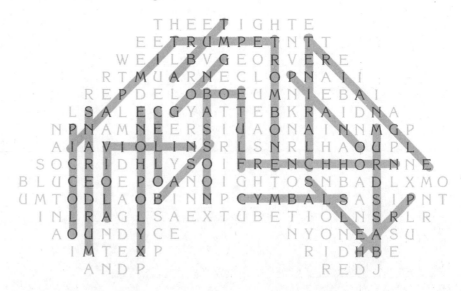

```
T H E E T I G H T E
E E T R U M P E T N T
W E I L B V G E O R V E R E
R T M U A R N E C L O P N A I I
R E P D E L O B O E U M N I E B A I
L S A L E C G Y A T T E B K R A I D N A
N P N A M N E E R S I U A O N A I N N M G P
A I A V I O L I N S R L S N R L H A O U P L
S O C R I D H L Y S O I F R E N C H H O R N N E
B L U C E O E P O A N O I G H T O S N B A D L X M O
U M T O D L A O B I N N P C Y M B A L S A S I P N T
I N L R A G L S A E X T U B E T I O L N S R L R
A O U N D Y C E                 N Y O N E A S U
I M T E X P                     R I D H B E
A N D P                         R E D J
```

# Puzzle Answers

## Saving Stamps • Page 82

## Having a Ball • Pages 84–85

*GOLF BALL*

*TENNIS BALL*

*BASKETBALL*

## Take Me Out to the Ballgame • Page 86

The extra letters spell out this joke:
Why did the baseball player blink his eyelashes
all day? Because he needed batting practice!

## Hit the Slopes • Page 87

## Scramble • Page 89

KIRN = RINK
LOGA = GOAL
OCLKC = CLOCK
SOTH = SHOT
TAKES = SKATE
CIE = ICE
TICKS = STICK
DROBA = BOARD
CHEBN = BENCH
KUPC = PUCK
ULOF = FOUL

## Spelling Ball • Page 90

Here are some of the words you can find in the "Spelling Ball":

| | | |
|---|---|---|
| ALIVE | OVER | SILVER |
| EVIL | PALE | SLIVER |
| LAP | PALER | TOIL |
| LEAP | PERT | TON |
| LION | PET | VELVET |
| LIVE | REAL | VETO |
| LIVER | REAP | VISION |
| NOISE | REAPER | VOTE |
| NOT | RELIVE | VOTER |
| NOTE | REVOTE | PAL(S) |
| OIL | SEAL | SLAP |

The ten-letter bonus word is TELEVISION.

## Swim Meet • Page 88

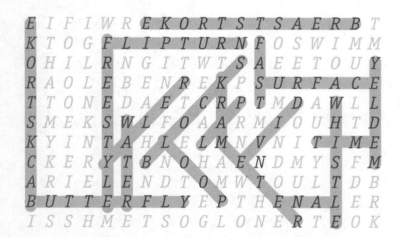

# Puzzle Answers

## Secret Soccer • Page 90

```
S R O S O S O C C E
O O R O S O C C E S
C E C C O C C O R O
C S O C E C E S O C
R O S E R E R O S S
S S O C C O S E O O
O C C S O C E C C E
C E R O C O C C E
C O O C S E O O S E
E C O S R O C C O S
```

## Floor Exercise • Page 91

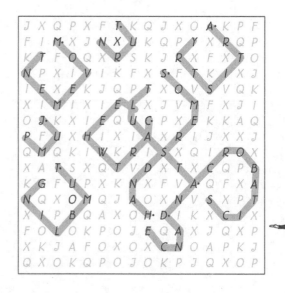

## Fully Equipped • Pages 92–93

ARCHERY
BASEBALL
BASKETBALL
FOOTBALL
KAYAKING
LACROSSE
SKATEBOARDING
ICE SKATING
BIKING
SOCCER
TENNIS
WEIGHTLIFTING

## Extreme Sports • Page 94

# The EVERYTHING KIDS' Word Search Puzzle and Activity Book

**Beautiful Ballerina • Page 96**

```
    É U
  S T Q J R W I A
L O E U I T T É J O
E T T E U O R I P E S Q
É O L A J É M P T W U A E
T S J R B A M S E Q E E C L
  E I A P O I N T E S U I O E U
L E O T A R D E O Q E S L I T E K
  O B U A R A B E S Q U E P R T O P
    I T I O N S M U S M L R U É S O
    É O R I P U I E L A T Q P I
    N T S É Q N I B Q É I O
        P O S I T I O N S
            Q S Y
```

**Funny Fairy • Page 97**

```
F E M A L E
S T A I N D
F K G E R U
L W I N G S
Y B C E L T
S M A L L L
```

STINKERBELL!

# Puzzle Answers

## Knight Night • Pages 98–99

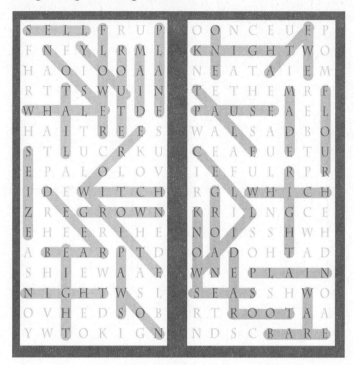

## Presto Chango • Page 100

WAND     SCARF
BUNNY    CARDS
FLOWER
STAR
HAT
ROPE

## Unusual Unicorn • Page 101

Special clothes that identifies a team = U N I F O R M
All of outer space and everything in it = U N I V E R S E
All the people in your city or town = C O M M U N I T Y
Imaginary animal with one horn = U N I C O R N
Gathering of old classmates = R E U N I O N
Long shirt that hangs to the knees = T U N I C
One-wheeled bike = U N I C Y C L E
Common summer plant with trumpet-shaped
   flowers = P E T U N I A
To join together = U N I T E
Only one of its kind = U N I Q U E

## Pirate Booty • Page 102

1. SILVER
2. PEARLS
3. GOLD
4. SAPPHIRES
5. EMERALDS
6. DIAMONDS
7. RUBIES

**Marvelous Mermaids • Page 103**

Mermaids are <u>LOVELY</u> fish-women that live <u>UNDERWATER</u> in the <u>OCEAN</u>. They have a <u>TAIL</u> instead of legs, and can <u>SWIM</u> really fast. <u>LEGEND</u> says that mermaids can <u>ENCHANT</u> sailors when they <u>SING</u>

**Ask an Alien • Page 104**

The words you are looking for:
LEADER, PLANETS, SPACESHIP, STARS, TECHNOLOGY, UNIVERSE, LIGHTS

The letters UFO appear in the puzzle grid ten times.

Greetings, Earthling!

WOW!

# Puzzle Answers

**Custom Castles • Page 105**

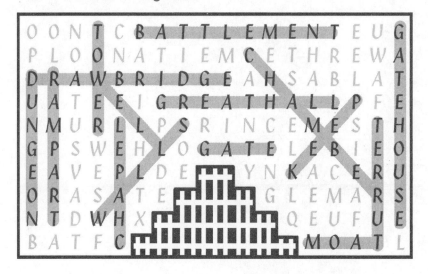

```
O O N T C BATTLEMENT E U G
P L O O N A T I E M C E T H R E W A
DRAWBRIDGE A H S A B L A T
U A T E E I GREATHALL P F E
N M U R L L P S R I N C E M E S T H
G P S W E H L O GATE L E B I E O
E A V E P L D E Y N K A C E R U
O R T A S A T E G L E M A R S
N T D W H X Q E U F U E
B A T F C MOAT L
```

**Dragon Breath • Page 106**

# The EVERYTHING KIDS' Word Search Puzzle and Activity Book

Look Again! • Page 108

1. Perfect Pets

2. Driveway Fun

3. You're It!

4. Savings Sum

5. Gearing Up

6. Farm Fun

crease folds
with thumbnail

7. Origami Animals

8. Floor Exercise

9. Dragon Breath